C000145437

GEOFF THOMPSON

Everything that Happens to Me is Fantastic

summersdale

EVERYTHING THAT HAPPENS TO ME IS FANTASTIC

Summersdale Publishers Ltd
46 West Street
Chichester
West Sussex
PO19 1RP
UK

www.summersdale.com
www.geoffthompson.com

Printed and bound in Great Britain

ISBN: 978-1-84024-768-8

Substantial discounts on bulk quantities of Summersdale books are available to corporations, professional associations and other organisations. For details telephone Summersdale Publishers on (+44-1243-771107), fax (+44-1243-786300) or email (nicky@ summersdale.com).

To my beautiful wife Sharon,
still the girl of my dreams twenty years in

Wheel-locked Boy

A fire in the speckled dark, later a violent sky of smoke.

★★★

An arrow of light from an unfamiliar window.

A cold dread growing, urging me home to mum.

I was only twelve.

The dread became a hand, heavy fingers nervous and trembling, searching for something precious and virginal to steal. First on my bare thigh, then advancing carefully inside cloth pyjamas, unbuttoned quietly by the thief as I slept.

Waking into an inferno.

Stilled by my own terror, startled by my own silent scream.

Only my hand would move.

As though it had its own existence independent of this wheel-locked boy. My hand lifted the greedy fingers as quietly as my terror would allow and placed their weight away from harm, then spent a long, dark life blocking its persistent advance, praying for an end, knowing no end would come.

I didn't tell anyone about my fire in that speckled night for fear of worse abuse from those that judge.

But later... as a wheel-locked man, the fire had grown inside me too big and smoke escaped and filled my sky with dark.

And then I told you... and you pretended that I'd made a lie. Maybe because you were afraid that the flames would jump like electricity and lick you, or maybe some shame found your bones and threatened to burn you more.

I don't know.

Only that I told you, and your denial turned my fire volcanic and I vomited a battalion of flaming rocks into ten dark ages of violence, leaving dead lava statues in my wake.

Later, my shadow spent, I was able to transmute my rage into ink and litter my world instead with an army of word disciples that march into a clearing sky.

Also by Geoff Thompson

Red Mist
Watch My Back: The Geoff Thompson Autobiography
The Elephant and the Twig: The Art of Positive Thinking
The Great Escape: The 10 Secrets to Loving Your Life and
Living Your Dreams
Fear – The Friend of Exceptional People: Techniques in
Controlling Fear
Shape Shifter: Transform Your Life in 1 Day
The Formula: The Secret to a Better Life
Stress Buster: How to Stop Stress from Killing You
Dead or Alive: The Choice is Yours
Everything That Happens to Me is Good
Everything That Happens to Me is Great
The Beginner's Guide to Darkness

Contents

Foreword...9

Introduction..12

Embodiment..15

Mind-forged Manacles.....................................19

Universal Orchestration...................................22

Call to Arms...24

The Hidden Place...27

Cunt!...30

The £250,000 Golf Ball...................................34

The Processional Effect...................................39

Everything that Happens to Me is Fantastic..........44

The 200-bit Reality..53

Flapping..58

The Mouse Leading the Camel.......................61

Halfway Up My Life...67

In the Room..76

Under the Bed in a Biscuit Tin........................82

The Many-failed Soul......................................95

Kissing Lepers..98

Participating Anthropic Principle..................104

I Am My Only Enemy, I Am My Only Friend....109

Slings and Arrows...115

Ten Thousand Angels......................................117

Gospel..122

Buccaneering Rabbits..125

The Left-hand Path..130

Small Profundities..134

Looking for the Ampersand..136

Writer..140

Further Reading..143

Foreword

'I am telling you this stuff to remind myself.' This is a phrase any attendee of a Geoff Thompson masterclass or seminar will be familiar with. It is a humble statement that Geoff paraphrased from the motivational guru Zig Ziggler. The essence of it speaks of a project in continual development. For Geoff Thompson, ex-abused child, ex-factory worker, ex-browbeaten husband, ex-brickie, ex-failed playwright, ex-rejected author, ex-doorman and ex-self-pitying blamer, everything is about the journey.

The articles you are about to read are notes taken from this journey. They provide the scaffolding around whatever major work Geoff is currently producing. However, do not expect a clinically planned structure. Unlike many philosophies you will read under the 'self-help' section of your local bookshop, the processes here mimic life in all its unpredictability, and describing them as 'journey notes' is very apt.

Each piece is a self-contained work that varies from the topical 'The Hidden Place' to more biographical articles, such as the self-reflective 'Halfway Up My Life'. Likewise, Geoff's sources for inspiration are unashamedly eclectic. He is clearly drawn to Dante's *Divine Comedy* and regularly cites it in much of his work, but he is equally happy to dedicate a whole article to Richard Adams' allegorical children's story *Watership Down* in 'Buccaneering Rabbits'.

His writing style varies too. 'Embodiment' makes a similar statement about what a single person can do, no matter their disadvantages, as in 'Gospel' and 'In the Room'. Each chapter demonstrates the conflict that Geoff has come across at every step of his journey. From the internal conflicts that have influenced him to write so prolifically about fear and the physical conflicts he fought on the nightclub doors that inspired his no-nonsense approach to martial arts to the bigger battles he has and will continue to face against his critics.

Geoff the philosopher embraces confrontation as though it were a piece of metaphorical gym equipment that he pumps to develop more motivational strength and purpose. However, Geoff the artiste is perhaps more vulnerable, as revealed in such pieces as 'Looking for the Ampersand'. And yet through showing the soft underbelly of the powerful armour-plated juggernaut that is Geoff Thompson the successful multi-discipline martial artist, the best-selling author, the BAFTA-winning playwright and the screenplay writer of a major motion picture, access to the success is granted to anybody. However, in order to really gain access to this journey we have to, as Geoff puts it, 'leave our excuses at the door'.

Jamie Clubb
February 2009

Introduction

You may have picked this collection of words up in a shop and thought, 'Why should I read this book?' Perhaps if I can tell you why I wrote this book, it might help you to see why you should invest a little of your time and a fraction of your money in reading it.

This has been a good year for me and my beautiful wife Sharon. Man, it has been exciting, and we are only five weeks in. We started the year (2009) with a bang! We released our very first feature-length film for cinema (*Clubbed*). This has been a fifteen-year project, so January felt a bit like landing on the moon after years of sky gazing and rocket building. We had three red carpet premieres, one in Leicester Square, London (we were papped – how delightful!), one in Broad Street, Birmingham, where hundreds attended and the press were there in force, and a third in Paris,

France, where we could not walk a hundred yards without bumping into a life-sized poster of *The Club* (as the Parisians had renamed it). It was a wonderful feeling standing at the Arc de Triomphe looking at a huge poster of our film. And what made it all the more exciting was the fact that my children were there to see it with me. I'd been telling them since they were babies (they are all adults now) that *one day your dad's film is going to be on at the pictures*, and now, suddenly, here we were, in a Paris cinema and receiving a standing ovation from an appreciative crowd.

It is one thing telling your children about the possibility of impossible dreams, but when they can see the dream fully realised with their own eyes, they cannot doubt it.

As well as *Clubbed* the movie I am in early development on two television series, advanced development on two more feature films, have two books in the pipeline for publication this year and I have two stage plays, both placed with a London theatre. As well as this I have a Heathrow of other stacking projects (too many to list here) all waiting for their place to land.

I am not a perfect man, but I am a man of action. I do not sit and talk the good fight; I am always in one arena or another, I am constantly journeying to the next lofty goal, never resting on my laurels, and forever challenging myself in the ongoing purification process of life. And I am a man of sincere honesty. So, the words you are about to digest – my traveller's notes – are as true as they are tested. No room for hypothesis in this book or in my life. This is the elixir of my journey thus far. It is my hope that the words and the lessons might inspire, direct and – if you are on that point of tipping – perhaps they will give you the little nudge you need to go off the edge.

And in falling (as the poet Rumi said) you will be given wings.

So why should you read this book?

Because it might entertain, it will probably enlighten, it might even anger you – and it is entirely possible that it could change the course of your life.

Thank you for reading.

Geoff Thompson
Coventry, England. February 2009

Chapter 1

Embodiment

I worked in a factory. I swept floors. Now I am sitting in the Empire cinema, Leicester Square, London, watching the gala premiere (on the biggest screen in the capital) of my first feature film, *Clubbed*.

So don't tell me that it can't be done. It can be done. It is being done.

I was a nightclub bouncer in a beer-sticky Coventry bar where aspiration and ambition got clubbed like a beached seal. Now I am sitting in Cineworld, Broad Street, Birmingham, presenting the British premiere of my first full-length screenplay to hundreds of people.

So don't tell me that it can't be done. It can be done. It is being done.

I am standing with the cast and crew of *Clubbed* before tens of thousands of fans at the Birmingham

EVERYTHING THAT HAPPENS TO ME IS FANTASTIC

City football ground. It is half-time, the green turf is our red carpet and as a celebration of our film we are being presented with a *Clubbed* football shirt signed by all the players.

So... don't tell me that it can't be done. It can be done. It is being done.

I am sitting on a factory toilet surrounded by the hum of spinning lathes and the oil of hard labour and I am writing my first book (*Watch My Back*) using reporters' pads and a biro (with perfunctory chewed lid). I am writing about exploits experienced in my employ as a club bouncer. I don't own a typewriter; I don't even know anyone who owns a typewriter, so I have no conception yet of how to take my words from biro to presentable manuscript. I only know a compulsion that drives my coal-face experiences to the white-lined page – which I follow. Later, after much disappointment and rejection I got the book published and now it has a global audience.

So don't tell me: 'It can't be done!' It can be done. It is being done.

I am at the French premiere of *Clubbed*. We are in love-capital Paris. The film has played in dubbed French and the audience are giving a standing ovation.

This film was born in oil and shit and now we are here, in the culture and fashion capital celebrating its fruition, so don't tell me that it cannot be done. It can be done. It is being done.

I am sitting in my front room and my chest is an accordion of sobs that are as savage as a football hooligan. I am reading a vitriolic 'script appraisal' (fifteen pages of spleen-vent that is writhing in ire) of my first attempt at a screenplay (in 1997) and the words stab like a death row injection.

Now I am at the BAFTA ceremony lifting a heavy mask before the world and thanking God for my first major award.

So don't tell me that it can't be done. It can be done. It is being done.

I am sitting on the stairs of my too small abode with its worrying repayments and I am reading my latest rejection letter with the unkind PS: 'Not sure who would want to read a book about a Coventry bouncer!'

Now I sit here with over 300,000 sales, hundreds of published articles, and a plethora of commissioned and acted stage plays, front cover profiles, a TV series, film deals, book contracts and awards.

Apparently a lot of people want to read about a Coventry bouncer!

So please, please do not tell me that it cannot be done. It can be done. It is being done.

I am telling you that success is a choice, not a lottery.

I am showing you that the dream is possible for all, not just a small minority

I am the embodiment.

You don't have to be a great talent (talent will develop), you just need to be a tenacious warrior, a man who is scared, but not frightened of being scared, a woman who is sensitive, but who does not cower and hide from sensitivity, a person who is in trembling awe of their potential, but who marinates in that awe.

An artist who gets knocked down by criticism seven times, but gets up for the eighth time.

Don't, please don't try to tell me that it cannot be done.

It can be done.

Man, it is being done!

Chapter 2

Mind-forged Manacles

Isn't this a wonderful time?

As I write, the news is spilling with talk of cutbacks and recession and disappearing capital and suicidal brokers, but I just keep thinking... isn't this a wonderful, purifying, catalytic time! A time to create and re-create, a time to produce and re-produce, a time to burn off the redundant and the spent as we rocket through the white-hot stratosphere of new possibilities.

People are worried.

Good! Worry is a fuel, it can be utilised.

People are frightened.

Great! There's nothing like fright to shake up the complacent norm and add a little turbo to positive action.

People are terrified.

Terror? Wow! Now we are talking. Now, my agitated friends, we are cooking up new possibilities on *Gas Mark 9*. Nothing stirs the soul and fires the spirit like a sprinkle of terror on your morning cornflakes. It gets people off the settee, it gets folk out of their made-for-the-bigger-person comfy-chair, it places a rocket up the arse of the old, tired, uninspired lives.

Man, what a *fucking* amazing time this is.

We are watching history unfold. We are history unfolding.

Recessionary times create revolutionary ideas. Recessionary times give birth to revolutionary people. Recession is the precursor to great innovation.

Did you know that the entire multi-billion-dollar film industry in the USA was born out of the Great Depression in the 1920s?

Out of the last recession we had here in the eighties my friend, John Harrison, built a multi-million-pound business on a start up fund of £500.

My other friend, Mike Liptrot, was made redundant as an electrician at the same time and he was scared; he ploughed his fear of penury into Judo. Today he is one of the top coaches in the world. *In the world!*

The whole of the Ford car empire only started because Ford was passionate (driven even) about manufacturing a vehicle that was affordable for everyone.

You (yes you!) have been looking for a burst of energy for a very long time, you have wanted out of your spent existence for as long as you can remember, and wasn't it only last Christmas (and the Christmas before that, ad infinitum) that you announced *It is time to change!* only to abandon the notion on 2 January when the 'entrepreneurial spirit' got mugged and left for dead by the hangover of Christmas past?

Man, this is such an amazing time. There has never been a better time to brush the cobwebs off your old dreams and air them in the light of new possibilities. There has never been a better time to break the cry of woe and instead use the cry in battle against those *mind-forged manacles*. For the resigned man there has never been a better time for renaissance.

The good life is not a lottery! Do not doubt me on that. The good life is a choice, and that choice is often made in times of inferno. And the current climate is offering all the start-up energy and all the incentive and all the fear that you need to make it so.

There has never been a better time.

And with 'the inferno' still very much in mind, let me leave you with the words of Dante because you need to hear them and you need to hear them today, as there was never a better time.

'Now is the time to rouse yourself',
The master said; 'for sitting on a cushion
Is not the way to fame, nor staying in bed.'

Chapter 3

Universal Orchestration

I wanted strong influences for my writing. I wanted to be around the best people on this spinning globe in order to inspire the development of my work. I told my wife Sharon, 'I'm going to ask Debi [my literary agent] to try to set up a meeting for me with Paul Abbot [a world renowned screenwriter].'

'Don't try to set up a meeting with Paul Abbot, stay at home and make your work shine, and Paul Abbot will be drawn into your orbit,' Sharon replied.

I said, 'Jimmy McGovern. He's a wonderful writer. I should try to meet him; he would be a great influence.'

She said, 'Do the work, Geoff! Make your words startlingly good and Jimmy McGovern will want to meet you.'

I said, 'I love Ken Loach! I am going to try to arrange a meet with him.'

'Don't try and arrange anything,' Sharon said, 'other than your written words on the screen, and arrange them so beautifully that Ken Loach will not only want to meet you, he'll ring you himself to tell you.'

So I stopped trying to force nature; I put my diary away and took off my go-faster stripes and I sat down to write. And I sat down for many thousands of hours over the weeks, months and years to come, and learned to script my words until they shone, until they were startling, until they were positively beautiful.

Paul Abbot invited me to his home for several script consultations; Jimmy McGovern came to see my play at the Liverpool Everyman theatre and called it a powerful piece of work; and Ken Loach, after seeing one of my short films, rang me at home and invited me to tea.

When you do the work you will not have to arrange meetings with the giants, the universe will orchestrate it all for you.

Chapter 4

Call to Arms

This is a time to bear arms; this is a time to wage war.

Now is the very moment that we should strip the yellow streak from our backs and face down our fears.

Aren't you tired of running scared?

Haven't you had enough of that bullying fear stamping on your dreams?

How long are you going to live under the dominion of anxiety?

Listen, your gold is just over the hill, beyond that crest of fear.

Your success is hanging like a ripe apple waiting to be plucked from the tree.

Your diamond chest is buried, just inches below your own feet.

There is only one thing stopping you from realising your dreams. Fear!

So hear me, hear me loud, heed my sage counsel, follow my suggestion; if the apple is your fruit, if the gold is your heritage and the success your birthright, if the buried diamonds are in your earth and fear is the only thing standing between you and it, why not – and this might seem radical – go out there and attack your fears, hunt your fears down, and be unflinching when you face your fears head on.

Be a warrior.

Gird your loins.

Bear your arms.

Push through the miasma of depression and gain clarity from your courage.

There has never been a greater illusion than fear.

Fear exists only whilst you believe in it – whilst you fear it.

So... stop believing, stop fearing.

Set up a shadow inventory, write down all your fears and set out on your warrior path.

Make this your life purpose and channel your fears into positive action and success.

Stop fucking about and building up fear with your unschooled thought. Instead, lend your thought to might. Invest your attention in divine purpose.

What is divine purpose?

To create an inner light for yourself by dissolving shadow.

And when you dissolve the shadow of one man you light a beacon for all men.

Start now.

Any delay, any thought of delay, any putting off until tomorrow what should be done today is the very beginning of failure.

Action has power. It has boldness. It excites God into action. It triggers universal orchestration, and guidance will come to you from any and every quarter.

Now is the time, my friend, to raise yourself above the parapet of ordinariness, to become extraordinary.

If you want extraordinary, be extraordinary and craft your own work of art.

You.

Be well.

Chapter 5

The Hidden Place

Ladies and gentlemen, boys, girls and creatures (all beautiful) of the world, you have witnessed history unfolding. Barack Obama, that wonderful statesman of courage and colour, has added a splendid dash of black to the American house of white. And in doing so he has sent the world an invitation to bring out their seed-dreams from that hidden place and plant them now, in the receptive soil of a new world. We now know that dreams can grow. The kin of slaves has taken the most powerful seat in the world of men and he has prepared a dream banquet and we are all invited. But there is a caveat! All of our names are on the list, but we are urged to leave our excuses at the door. Excuses are against the dress code of this black tie celebration, because excuses are out of vogue. We can no longer lament from hill and rooftop 'not for the likes of us'. If we are unhappy or unsuccessful or unfulfilled, let us not tilt the lance and blame our race or our colour or creed. That is too easy. That is too deliciously comfortable. If we are to stake our claim to fame, we must vacate the pillow and the bed and seek out, instead, growth in places of personal discomfort. And we cannot decry the gods for leaving us with uncharted terrain – Barack has lit a new path to success and he is inspiring us to follow. Even our historical penury must be crossed off the excuse list because the good and the great can and do come from anywhere. We now have the proof! And we can complain no more about not having the time. I've just had the final count in and it is official: Barack Obama only gets 24 hours in his one day. What a delightful coincidence, that's exactly the same number of hours that you and I get. (But how are we employing them?) Lack of privilege was always an ice-pick apology that could hack feet deep into the ice of rationalisation, but no more. No more. Where was Obama's privilege? His heritage is one without great advantage; his father was a goat herder. And please, you can forget prejudice. Our man of 'the now' has to preach his liberty from behind armour-plated glass.

As we speak, the dull and the ignorant and the downright evil conspire his assassination purely on the basis of ethnicity. And to those disabled of body, mind and spirit, let us not forget that the black race were disabled for many years; they had no liberty.

And please don't bring the spent pretext that spouse and children hold you back, whilst Michelle Obama prepares the White House for her family. Man, she is doing it, and in doing it she is giving us all permission to do it too. And lack of money? When your intent is focused, the cash will fall from the skies. Excuses are cinder, the ashes of the old guard pyre. And like the phoenix we can all rise out of the residue and be resurrected. So ladies, gents, boys and girls and creatures all, come to the party light of excuse, and instead of just witnessing history unfolding, why not join history, and unfold your very best self with it. Why not place your name and your namesake into the scroll of time? Our species has just added a splendid dash of black into the house of white and it has set us all free.

Chapter 6

Cunt!

I'd written a film (*Clubbed*) and found myself, after many years of hard work, finally sharing it with the world at a press junket in London. I was being interviewed by various leading newspapers and television companies to promote the film. I was talking with one reporter (who I really liked, he was a nice man) who looked slightly miffed. 'In this film,' he asked, more for himself, I suspect, than the paper he was writing for, 'in this film, do you use the C word?'

I presumed (and presumed correctly) that he was alluding to the word 'cunt', the use of which automatically gets you an 18 certificate in British cinemas.

Now my film is hard-hitting (all of my films are hard-hitting), it involves colourful characters making their way though a very dramatic, one might say, violent narrative. It is not about flower arranging, it is not a romcom, and it definitely is not an episode of *The Bill*. So... yes, the word 'cunt' is not only used (and I told him this) it is used frequently. But it is not really me that is using the words, I tried to explain, it is the characters. In the universe that these folk inhabit, 'fuck', 'cunt' and 'bastard' are used in everyday parlance. And if I don't allow them to use their usual parlance, then their world becomes a parody, which is not what I want to write.

He said, 'I have a friend, who is a very influential academic, very literary, who will not even watch a film if the C word is used.'

And?

'Well... he feels that the use of such words is lazy, gratuitous and violent. And he won't be any part of it.'

I found this interesting, especially because I was talking to a fellow artist, and art should never be about limitation or public opinion, it should be about inclusion and expression – individual expression.

It is about being brave and having bollocks, or (as they say in the game) 'an individual voice'.

Two things jumped immediately to mind here. 1) The word 'cunt' is just one of many thousands of words available for use in the English dictionary, and that word, in and of itself, cannot be lazy or gratuitous or violent (intent and context are responsible here,

31

and even then it is subjective). If you go back a century the word 'cunt' was not seen as offensive at all, in fact if you really wanted to offend a hundred years ago you would use the word 'cad' which, I think you will agree, is pretty tame compared with today's vocabulary. And you might also be surprised to know that early Shakespeare was riddled with expletives, which have been weeded out over the years by folk fearful of (fucking) offending. And 2) when the fuck did art start getting direction from public opinion?

I told my friend that if he was really concerned about offending friends (and family and influences), then he should visit his friends (and family and influences), make a list of all the words that they find offensive or distasteful, exclude them from his further articles and see what he is left with. That way he could be sure of not offending anyone he knew. But, I warned, if he did follow this tack, the work he produced would no longer be his own work, and what was left would be as bland as a magnolia-coloured wall.

And even a magnolia-coloured wall is going to offend some fucker.

My point is this: are we individuals expressing our life as individuals, or are we sheep, following the fashions and flavours and fancies of the masses, for fear of being out of favour? And this is much more important than the usage of a hated word or a banned phrase; this is about the jobs we take, the partners we choose and the very life we live. Who the fuck wants to live a hand-me-down existence, walking on egg shells through an inoffensive milieu with a magnolia partner on your arm? This is not your calling; this is not what you came here to do. This kind of life is hard labour, a prison without walls. And if this is the kind of banal life you are living then your life, my friend, is not an original existence, it is a pale, self-editing, cowardly facsimile of an original existence.

Perhaps now is the time to look at your life, the one where all the 'fucks' and 'cunts' have been edited out by external pressures, and start filtering them back in again.

I mean, at the end of the day, what is a life without a 'bastard', a 'wanker', or a 'fucking cunt'?

Chapter 7

The £250,000 Golf Ball

Tony was driving his smart Jaguar down a tight Coventry lane, just on the outskirts of the city, when it happened.

A sudden 'bang!' from out of the blue – the kind that has you pumping on the brake and screeching to a halt. Something, some foreign object, a projectile from outer space had hit the wing of his car at high speed.

Tony climbed out and headed straight to the front wing, driver's side, and there it was: a dent in the metal, a perfect indent the size of a... well... exactly the size of a golf ball. A quick scan of the area revealed the offending object sitting guiltily on the side of the road. A wider scan revealed a golf driving range just at the back of the lane.

Dent, golf ball, golf driving range! It all quickly fell into place.

Tony – a little pissed at the chock-sized dent in his prized vehicle – made his way straight over to the reception at the edge of the range. This should not (he thought) take long. He was on his way to a big business meeting so he didn't have a lot of time to spare that day, just enough to introduce himself to the manager of the course and perhaps exchange insurance details. He quickly sought out the man in question and presented him calmly and quietly and respectfully with the ball, the story, and the opportunity to make amends. He assumed that it would probably be a five minute chat, followed by a very small insurance claim, the golf range taking full responsibility. It was the only range for 10 miles, the lane was at the very bottom of the (too short) driving range and the ball had fallen out of the sky as he drove past. It was open and shut as far as Tony could see. And, let's be honest here, this was not a big incident, it was not life-threatening and certainly nothing to lose any sleep over. It was just a random accident involving a £2.50 golf ball and a small insurance claim.

Or was it? As it turned out, this was (perhaps) less of a random incident and more of a serendipitous occurrence. And, my friends, this turned out to be no mere £2.50 golf ball, neither was it a small insurance claim and an hour's bodywork from a local garage. This was (no less than) a voice from the sky, a divine orchestration, an opportunity of limitless proportions. It was a chance for the golf manager to do the right thing. A chance to be magnanimous. Actually, it was an opportunity for him to make lots of money. Certainly it was a chance for him to save lots of money, a quarter of a million pounds to be exact.

You see, Tony, as well as being my best friend, is also an international business man; his company makes tens of millions every year, a proportion of which, up until this day, they spent on entertaining their very wealthy clients at this particular golf resort, restaurant and hotel.

The manager didn't know this, of course. And Tony didn't feel the need to mention it; he was on his way to a meeting and didn't want to get caught up in unnecessary discourse, and certainly he did not want to use his business dealings with the resort as a bargaining tool. Tony didn't think that would be necessary. It was a small incident that he was sure the manager would deal with fairly and quickly.

So the manager did not know anything about Tony. All he knew for sure was that he had a gent in front of him looking to make a small claim on the company's insurance policy and... *he wasn't going to have any of it.* Not only did he deny any responsibility ('What makes you think the ball came from our range?' and 'Can you prove it?') he was also very disrespectful about it, informing Tony that there was no way he could prove the ball came from his range (please!) and that even if it did, he as the manager could not, and would not, bear any responsibility for it. He suggested that if Tony wanted to pursue the issue any further he should try to locate the member who (may or may not have) hit the offending ball and claim off him/her as an individual. This, of course, in a large golf club with hundreds of members, would be an improbable course of inquiry.

The issue here is less about who was actually at fault (the club or the member), but rather the matter of magnanimity. The manager, with his arrogant dishonesty and small-mindedness, lost the opportunity (one of many I would imagine, by his attitude) of creating wealth and inspiring goodwill by doing what is right. Instead he sent Tony away dissatisfied. So Tony did probably the only thing that was left open to him; he placed the matter in the hands of his company solicitor (he was driving a company car).

Next, Tony cancelled all of his many business dealings with the club; a projected fortune over the span of his career. And of course he put a stop to any future business dealings with the resort, which, looking at the exponential growth of Tony's company, would have added up to a great deal of money. Not to mention the fact that many of the associates Tony brought to the resort for meetings and meals were hugely influential themselves and would no doubt have used the complex for their own business dealings.

Tony did not do this out of spite or malice – I sensed no anger in his voice when he re-told the story – he said he just did not want, and could not afford, to be involved with a dishonest and disingenuous company.

Goodwill costs nothing at all, but it can reap a fortune when it is congruent. Honesty takes a lot of courage and faith, but in the end it sets you free. And magnanimity has the power to forge fast friends and fiscal opportunities that offer great and profitable longevity.

And the opposite could quite easily turn a £2.50 golf ball into a £250,000 liability (and in this case it did).

And who knows, if the golf manager had been a bit more open, a tad more generous, he may have even converted his poor business judgement into a very rich vein of friendship.

Chapter 8

The Processional Effect

Imagine if you will the common garden honey bee, hopping from flower to flower collecting pollen that he intends to take back to his hive family in order to feed the queen bee and sustain his friends and family.

A simple manoeuvre. A basic task. A solid, honourable, selfless purpose. 'Go out, young bee, and – similar to when Cuba Gooding Jnr screamed down the telephone at Jerry McGuire (in the film of the same name) – *"Show me the honey!"'*

The honey bee knows its purpose. It knows what it is doing.

Or does it?

What the honey bee does not know, what the honey bee could not know, is that in the process of travelling from plant to plant, from flower to flower, he inadvertently collects pollen on his tail and accidentally pollinates all the flowers and plants in an act so vital to the eco-structure of this spinning planet that mankind would perish without it.

The bee's purpose is simple and it is based on its hive instinct. But the processional effect of the bee's gathering is so massive that I am hardly able to articulate it with words.

Now, I want you to imagine another cross-pollinating processional effect that is equally mammoth and equally accidental and it all started with a race – one that was precipitated by fear.

The race in question was 'the Space Race', and it occurred between the Russian and American governments. The finish line? Man walking on the surface of the moon!

The premise of this race (or the belief) was that whoever landed a man on the moon first got to control space, and whoever gained control of space automatically held dominion over the earth. As I said, it was a race precipitated by fear and ignorance. I mean, who cares who got into space first? Do you? I don't give a horse's hoot. It does not excite me, it doesn't inspire me but... but, but, but what I do care about, what I am interested in, what does excite me, is the wonderful, paradigm-shattering by-product of that wacky race between the global behemoths.

Or what the visionary inventor Buckminster Fuller called 'the processional effect'.

As far as President Kennedy was concerned, he just wanted to place an American astronaut on the moon within a decade. He felt that this would bring back power-pollen to the American hive and ensure its survival in a war that was freezer-box-cold cold. What Kennedy did not realise, what Kennedy could not have realised, was that America, at that time in history, did not have the technology to place a man on the moon. It was discovered that, in order to meet Kennedy's weighty directive and place moon dust on the boot-soles of Armstrong within ten years, they would have to leave the cutting edge of current technology and venture out onto the bleeding edge of the unknown and undiscovered, where imagination meets creation and where creation launches mankind into a new era.

To satisfy outrageous demands one, of course, has to go to outrageous lengths. In other words, in order for *man and moon* to marry, they had to invent and create new technology (now known as *space technology*). In fact, it is said that in order for President Kennedy to bring his 'one small step' into mankind's reality, 1,000,000 (that is **one million**) new pieces of technology had to be invented by the current crop of scientists.

1,000,000!!!!

Kennedy could not have known (surely) that his space dream would change the course of mankind forever. The by-product of the technology that built a ship capable of space travel was and is the mobile phone you are carrying on your hip right now, the computer at your desk, the engine in your car. In fact, pretty much every new and exciting piece of technological, life-enhancing piece of kit that you and I absolutely take for granted on a daily basis can be traced back to that race for space.

Aiming for the moon changed the earth almost beyond recognition, because the processional effect, the cross-pollination (although accidental) was so very far reaching.

The race for space inspires me to aim equally high in my own life. If, for instance, I aim to be a millionaire, or billionaire, or BAFTA winner, or recipient of an Oscar, or any other such global goal, how many things will I have to learn, how many skills will I have to master, what bleeding edge human extensions will I need to imagine and create in order to make my goal a living reality? And in creating those new tools, how many individuals peripheral to my singular intention, my original schematic, will benefit from my example as I have benefited from the examples set before me, either with the inspiration it fed me or the proven path it created? Equally important, who will be inspired to aim high, win and create by your aspirational conquests?

Often we are motivated to achieve by desirous longing or by buck-naked terror and we, in the throws of creation, probably think our efforts are personal and autonomous. But we all need to know that everything we do has an effect on everything and everyone else, and whilst our singular purpose might just be to bring home the honey, the processional effect is so vast, so grand, so earth-shatteringly vital that all of mankind will be elevated by it. And with that as your motivation I think it only right that you think, that you talk and that you do BIG. That way, you ensure that the by-product of your worthy labour and your joyful creation will encourage labour worthy enough to inspire joy in all creation.

Chapter 9

Everything that Happens to Me is Fantastic

I was so ill that I thought I might be dying. Honestly, I exaggerate not. To the outside world I looked fine; I did not stop working, I did not stop taking calls. I put my best face on and fronted the world bravely. But, inside, something was passing over. Inside it was kicking off like a crammed nightclub on a balmy night.

Mentally I was crawling on all fours, moving very little, and praying a lot.

I could tell you that I was dissolving because my beautiful dad was dying of cancer at the time, and that the loneliness and fear and pain playing out in his eyes tipped me – and it did tip me – but it wasn't that.

Well, let's just say that it wasn't just that.

I could also tell you that I was knocked off balance by two years of polishing a very personal stage play extolling my violent past, a savage catharsis that allowed me to exhume some ugly demonic archetypes, place them on a stage and invite audiences to judge me.

Or I could tell you that the cause was the fifteen-year journey of structuring a screenplay about my struggles through depression, turned into a major and painful atonement.

Or even that forty-seven years of personal purification, evicting shadows that fought a pitched and bloody battle to keep their residency, was finally taking its toll... but I won't because, whilst it did knock me off balance, investing so much of myself into projects that I struggled to bring to fruition, it was not ultimately this that threw me over the edge.

Well, let's just say that it wasn't *just* this that nudged me over the precipice.

My body looked all right to the larger world, but let me tell you that it didn't feel so splendid living inside an imploding mass of fleshy spaceship. My mind was impaired by multifarious struggles, and my internals churned like an industrial mincer. My bladder felt ravaged from an overworked and oversensitive nervous system (either I could not piss, or I could not stop pissing, and there was not an hour or a minute of the day when I did not feel the urge to piss, even on my long-distance runs, even in my sleep, even when there wasn't a fluid ounce inside of me to vacate). I was sent to the hospital and tested for everything: prodded, poked, scrutinised and fingered. Sometimes it was by male doctors who searched for cancers in my most personal cavities, but never once engaged my mental anguish, and at other times it was by female doctors who had more empathy for the chair I sat on than they did for me, and occasionally, very occasionally, I was embraced by wonderful human beings who offered love and concern.

Some suggested that my pain was a symptom of trying to die for my dad (he had prostate cancer). And, man, I did feel like dying for my dad, even though I innately knew that a thousand sacrificial deaths would not spare my dad even one night of torment.

Others said I was a 'burn-out', the victim of too much ambition and more work than my body could tolerate. More still suggested that I over-thought, over-fucking-sympathised and over-indulged my empathy for the pain of the world.

All of which is true.

But none of which plunged me through all nine circles of Dante's abyss.

Well, let us say that all of these elements played cameos in my demise, but none had the leading role.

I knew what was wrong with me, and it would not be discovered in a blood test or an internal examination of my flesh.

The reason I was dying, the cause of my implosion, the root to my psychosomatic illness (that had manifested as a physical agony) came down to one thing: I was scared. Terrified actually. Of losing my wife!

I was not scared of losing in a fight. Let me be clear about that. And body parts were not on the list of things I feared losing either. A ravaged ear, a broken nose, distorted fingers pointing hideously in the wrong direction – merely war wounds from the battles I'd waged with life. In my Neanderthal period I had been in dozens of microcosmic wars on sticky nightclub carpets and on neon-lit pavements outside late night chip shops, and with some killers too. Tooth and nail I fought, my lacerated and bulbous knuckles a record of every match, my scarred face a testimony to every caught blow.

No, I did not fear losing in a fight.

I was not afraid, interestingly, of losing my good health, only inasmuch as it might contribute to me losing my good wife. What young, desirable woman would want to carry an ailing male not capable of fighting, fucking or feeding the family (and all those other jobs that men think that women think are important)?

I was not afraid of illness, not even a terminal one. Cancer and its cohorts could go and fuck themselves for all I cared. Death held no fear for me either. Honestly. Only... only if I had cancer and had to spend time in hospital, where a man cannot perform his role and function as a breadwinner, surely my wife would betray me, abandon me, leave me for some healthy virile mate with a backbone; someone... what's the word? Worthy. Someone worthy! And if I was dead, man, there is no way I could be dead; that would entail separation from my wife and that was a fear too big to even contemplate.

Cancer was only feared because it created a temporary separation (and vulnerability), and death only had one sting for me – losing Sharon.

This is what tipped me.

Although, it wasn't really about losing Sharon. It was not about being betrayed by Sharon, nor abandoned. She was merely the focus of my fear, and if I was married to Jesus Christ himself the fear would have been no less potent, because the fear was in the world of me, not in the world of men. Me and Sharon were as tight as a folk singer's fringe. We were together all the time and there was no hint, premonition or real threat of separation. Consciously I felt ridiculous; I was a grown man, I had four grown children, and me and Sharon had been together (at the time) for seventeen years. I also felt selfish and narcissistic. Or should I say, a part of me felt like this. My fear may seem silly, even ludicrous, looking from the outside in, but to me it was as terrifying as climbing out of a dugout with a rifle, bayonet fixed, and rushing into the no-man's land of mortal combat. I realised that this fear had been in me for as long as I could remember, certainly it was there before me and Sharon, but because it had been left untreated it had grown and was now bursting out of my seams.

At the point of toppling I felt as though I was dying. My body reacted as though I was dying. And I knew without hesitation that if I didn't deal with this growing demon soon, it was surely going to deal with me.

I was suffering from what psychologists call an 'abandonment schema'. Even though and even when everything and everyone around me held a safe assurance that I would not be abandoned, I always, always, always thought I would. A growing, greedy, ravenous part of me actually knew I would. To overcome this fear, to dissolve it, I had to let go of that part. The frightened child inside me that had been sexually assaulted and emotionally abandoned was the cause of all my pain, and he was also the key to all the freedom I could ever wish for. And no matter how many times people assured me and reassured me that I was safe and that I would not be abandoned, and that actually there is no such thing as abandonment, my fear still grew until my skin was too tight for it and was in danger of rupturing.

The solution was to let go. Let go.

Let go of the need for assurance and reassurance.

Let go of the false belief that I could be abandoned.

Let go of the childish need for certainty.

Let go of the false belief that I would not cope without my wife.

Let go of the need for clarity.

Let go of the false belief that I was not worthy.

Let go of Sharon!

Excuse me!!!! Are you fucking mad? What are you saying? Let go of Sharon?

You can fuck right off.

Let go. Let go of Sharon.

Even the words voiced in the safety of my own head were an abomination.

Fuck off!

Let her go.

Didn't you hear what I said? Did you not hear the word I used (and not lightly let me tell you)? ***I am terrified!***

Underlined, bold and in italics (if you don't mind).

And, I might add, massively ashamed of my terror.

I have always been a warrior (I told myself unconvincingly); I thrive on uncertainty.

So why can't I let go? At the time I was not even capable of saying the words out loud. I kid you not. It took me weeks and weeks of knee-wobbling anticipation before I could voice the words and even then, when I did, it was done quickly and sodden in sulk, like a teenager forced to make an apology to a parent.

I let go of Sharon.

The turning point for me came because of two things. 1) My fear had become so potent that my body could no longer contain it at the same time as staying healthy. And 2) I am a warrior. That is what I am. It is how I live. It is how I have always been. At school I faced down my bullies in the yard and on the field after classes. And as a young adult I chased away depression by becoming a hunter of shadows. I have always prided myself on the fact that I will not be bullied, not by people, not by out-of-control emotions and definitely not by irrational and untrue fears.

There can be no bigger illusion than fear.

So I let go of Sharon. I dropped her like a brick that was very hot.

And here lies the revelation: in letting go of Sharon – who I feared losing more than my own life – I also automatically let go of the need to own, direct and control everything else inside and outside of my life.

Everything!

And I realised that in letting go I became free. And I became happy and so fucking light I nearly floated. And I discovered something wonderful; the things we cling onto control us, they actually imprison us. And when we let go we get to control the whole world.

When I was going through this scalding experience I just kept saying to myself (especially when the letting go was killing me), 'This is good, this is great, actually, this is fucking fantastic!'

And it was fantastic, it is fantastic, and in the future, when I have to let go of more fears and the experience is a painful purification, it will be fantastic again.

Everything that happens to me is fantastic.

★★★

As a postscript I have to tell you that the letting go was gradual, but the results were profound. And, as irony would have it, the more I let go of my wife, the closer we became. And I have never been so in love in my life.

Chapter 10

The 200-bit Reality

There has never been a better time to invest in yourself.

The morning, dinner time and evening news are all telling us the same thing: as I write, the financial situation is dire; there is no money about; we are in a recession.

Is it true?

Yes, of course it's true.

Well, partly true.

Let me explain.

Contemporary psychologist Mihali Chicksent-mihalyi (author of *The Flow*) said that, at any one time, there are about 4,000,000 bits of information trying to inform us about the world, but our brains are only able to process about 200 of them at once, so the reality we experience is true (recession, doom and gloom), but only partially true. If the 200 bits of information we are processing are all accessed from the news, the newspapers and the word of our (well -meaning but negative) friends and family, and they are all talking recession, then of course our reality – our very small 200-bit reality – is going to be focussed on recession. If, however – like me – you choose not to watch the (bad) news, morning, noon and night, and instead look further afield for your sustenance, you may be looking at a 200-bit horse of an entirely different colour.

Reality is being created and recreated, underlined and underscored, hashed and rehashed with every new bit of data we receive and process.

There is no money out there, the analysts say. *It has all gone!*

Has it really gone?

Of course it hasn't *really* gone, it has simply moved. *Somewhere else.*

Our job is to find that *somewhere else*, and we do this, first, by changing the information that we digest as a daily staple. Stop accepting and processing the same statistics as everyone else and start searching for the information (that is out there, that has always been out there and that will always be out there) that offers a road map with a multitude of paths filled with abundant opportunities.

The information we are being offered currently is creating a lot of fear in people. And fear (of course) triggers the fight/flight/freeze syndrome.

Rather than look objectively at the news, we try and fight it, we run away from it or we simply freeze in terror and accept the inevitable.

I believe fear can be a good thing. It can act as a catalyst. It can offer great purchase to those who want to dine on better fare, those who are tired of living under the dominion of limitation.

It can inspire (in me and you) massive action.

We do not have to accept the begging bowl of famine; we can go out there and discover our own feast.

There has *never* – I repeat, *never* – in the history of the world been a better time to invest in you.

Just because the majority want to paddle and peddle in misery, just because they choose (yes they do choose) to accept the dietary staple offered abundantly by media, and just because they decide to believe that the 200 bits of information (out of possibly billions) *is reality* (like believing that one line from one book, in a million libraries, is the gospel) does not make it true.

My friends, *my friends*... there has never been a better time to invest in yourself.

1) How do you start?
2) Where do you start?

3) What do you start?
4) Why do you start?

1) You start by accepting the gospel as reality and not as a scared and lonely line from a solitary book, and by believing the prophets, the saints, the mystics and the scientists. In this way we create and we recreate reality every day; our reality is but one room in a house of a million rooms. And by training ourselves to access new information we can ease ourselves into them all; we can even get out of the house.

2) Start here (this is information), raid the libraries, surf the rapids of the information highway, be a busy bee in the book shops – *Amazon will set you free*! Change your 200 bits of information daily by reading and watching and marinating in new data – there are people out there waiting to give it to you (many for free).

3) Act on the new information. Place a yoke around it and make it work for you. Make the changes in your life that will make the difference in your reality.

Everything is information!

The food you eat is information; it enters your body as a fuel and becomes part of your universe.

When you eat junk food, you are taking in information. But... it is junk.

When you gorge on the critical and the unkind that tabloids spew into your front rooms, know that they are more concerned with teasing your arousal with a car-exit knicker-shot than they are with informing you of your absolute and unquestionable ownership of limitless realities.

They offer information. But is it empowering?

Shit in, shit out.

When you are offered the current financial milieu (what you see, hear, smell, touch, intuit), know that you are being offered a sapling and not the forest.

4) You start because... man, there has never been a better time to invest in yourself.

And if you don't invest in yourself, who will?

This is your life. If you leave it to others they will simply feed, force or coerce you into living their reality. And where's the fun in that?

Chapter 11

Flapping

When the workers *in the world at large* take their wild cats out of the cage and march on the street with angry banners... I lock the cage, burn my banner and come back to me, the only place where demands are met and their solutions found.

When the world out there is flapping, I go inside and I tighten my own game.

When the lazy and the lost sit at home when they are capable of working, when they could be experiencing the joy of creation and an earned wage and the country buckles and staggers because they do not...

I stop being a voyeur, I stop myself from judging the path of other people, and instead add hours of labour to my own day, create more this week than last, and plan more for next week than this.

When the world out there is flapping, I go inside and I tighten my own game.

When the hypocrites pray in public and perv in private, when corrupt governments kill in macrocosm whilst demanding that the microcosm carry no arms, and when the world of men starts to mirror a world of menace...

I pray more in private and scorch every arm of personal perversion, I cease all killing, in thought and word and in deed and I demand nothing from others that I do not do myself...

When the world out there is flapping, I go inside and I tighten my own game.

When other cats are getting fat on spoils not shared and looking for comfort, when the usurers in banks and institutions pack their pockets with sinful gain and ease their conscience with small public donations...

I live lean and adopt massive generosity; I lean into life's sharp edges to curb my comfort and I give more than is asked and keep my philanthropy anonymous and private.

When the world out there is flapping, I go inside and I tighten my own game.

When society starts sinking deeper into the mire, and even our leader-saints start to look like heathen-sinners, and our media continues to serve Satan with its thinly disguised pornography...

Like Dante I set my sights for Beatrice, I lead my self with light and I starve Beelzebub by eschewing the gutter in the press.

When the world out there is flapping, I go inside and I tighten my own game.

When the sovereigns bring dishonour to their position, potentates eat their subjects into starvation and dictators imprison in the name of freedom...

I search for self-sovereignty, and I honour the pain of position, I feed all those in need of alms and I oust my inner dictator, so that anyone in my orbit shall know freedom through me.

When the world out there is flapping, I go inside and I tighten my own game.

Chapter 12

The Mouse Leading the Camel

Did you ever watch an interview with an obese government official talking about the health and fitness of our nation and think, 'But you're six stone overweight?'

Or did you ever make question marks with your eyebrows when a highly intelligent, fiscally successful politician talked on TV about the need for honesty and trust in government, only weeks after finishing a prison term for corruption?

Or better still, have you ever been astounded when spiritual behemoths (in the higher echelons of the church) are convicted in a court of law for paedophilia, while their seniors desperately try to cover up and lie to save papal embarrassment?

I think we have all experienced these anomalies.

The issue of people who are highly developed in one area and almost foetal in another has always massively intrigued me. The fact that you could have a man or a woman that is five stone overweight working as a school teacher or a headmaster or a doctor or politician is very puzzling. They understand enough about policy to be in office, looking after the welfare of perhaps thousands of people, yet they cannot look after the welfare of their own body. This is not to say that people who are not complete can't teach you anything. If that were the case none of us would be teachers, least of all me. I am still very imperfect and work every day to level my own hills and fill my own valleys. However, it should highlight the fact that we teach what we are, so it is important to work on our imperfections. Otherwise we will become, as the poet Rumi said, 'a mouse pretending to lead a camel'.

Intellectually they are highly developed, but physically and psychologically they are still in embryo.

Similarly, I know many people who are absolute artisans when it comes to physical culture, but are intellectual and spiritual dwarfs. I know many world-class martial artists who have no idea about finance and economics and many of them, believe it or not, have no spiritual development at all and hold onto their students like jealous husbands.

What I realised very early on in my own development was that if I was to become a free man I had to develop myself in all areas, starting with the very basic physical. This was my base camp. Then I delved into the psychological, physiological, biological, intellectual, and from there I explored truth and how truth was malleable and how information could change truth, how experience could change truth, how perception could change truth, and even how culture changed truth. After studying my own layers from the surface to the core I studied the ethical, the moral, the financial, the cultural and the environmental, I looked at class and caste, I took my bones to other areas of the world and then started to look *outside the house*. I realised that, as Alfred North Whitehead (an English mathematician who became a revered philosopher) said, truth did not only have 'simple location' but that Beauty, Truth and Goodness can be revealed to us as our ability to see becomes deepened through the rigours of practice.

Working on all these areas helped me to find my place spiritually. For me, the real ethereal treasures did not come until I had first exhausted the extremes of my corporeal body. I did this through very serious martial arts training. I went heavily into all-out knockout or submission fighting. This involved working heavily and at a high level in Judo, wrestling, boxing, karate, Chinese gung fu, Thai boxing and any other system that stretched me physically and psychologically. I even spent a decade working as a nightclub bouncer to stretch the limits of myself and dissolve my fear-blocks.

I found a higher consciousness through very hard contact.

When you push yourself to your physical and psychological limits it is hard not to bump into God. In fact, I would say that mastering of the corporeal develops you into a strong conduit for God. Gurdjieff discovered something similar – he found that we could not access what God had in store for us until we had first prepared ourselves through 'conscious labour and deliberate suffering'. My conscious labour was exhaustive physical conditioning. My deliberate suffering was mastering the senses via control of the palate. Ghandi believed that if you mastered the palate all the other senses fell into line, and once you mastered the senses you literally controlled the world.

I have cross-referenced this with my own intuition and my own experience and found it to be true.

Being a lifelong advocate of the martial arts I see things in very pragmatic terms; I always aim to get to the very top of whatever class I am in, and when I get there (and I always get there eventually) I then place myself at the bottom of someone else's class.

If you are not at the bottom of someone's class how are you going to grow?

I went inside myself and struck gold.

I realised that all the real bounty came when I courted the kind of discomfort that I knew would help me grow, when I stopped following other people's maps and started to follow my own. I became an alchemist and started to turn my discomfort, my pain, my fear, my jealousy, my envy, my greed, my lust, my joy, my happiness – all of my very strong emotions – into gold. I recognised that they were all the same at their core, they all came from the same place, in the centre they were all just energy looking to find form, all I had to do was learn to handle this energy and craft it into the shapes that pleased me most, and hopefully help others to do likewise.

The benefit of this kind of practice is that there is no room for spiritual bypassing! I find that people want to access the great before they have mastered the ordinary, which would be like being dropped on the peak of Everest without any acclimatisation. It would kill you. So for me, all things come through the physical; this route acted as a base camp from which I was able to access all the different levels until I found my own personal peak.

Of course, I married the heavy physical training with voracious reading, and – like the physical – I increased the level of books I read, starting with the easy-to-read, easy-to-find volumes that spoke in a basic language, books that inspired me to delve deeper, moving onto the more challenging reads, books that sometimes shattered my world view and challenged my sense of self.

But what was shattered I rebuilt, like the phoenix rising from its own ashes.

And any challenge to my sense of 'I' only told me that I had not yet found my sense of 'I', because I don't think that can be challenged.

My life thus far has been one of much colour, I have (as the Irish say) been around a few corners, and all of my learning has taught me how little I really know – and the realisation of knowing that there is too much to know is to know everything.

What I do know now for sure is that I never want to be a novice calling myself master. I have no intention of becoming a fat life-coach, an incongruent politician, or a religious hypocrite. And although I am certainly not a master yet, I definitely am not pretending, and certainly I am no mouse.

Chapter 13

Halfway Up My Life

When I was young and depressed and desperately looking for a new reality, I searched the book shops high and low for words that might offer me escape from my fears, or at the very least a little balm to sooth the scalding sear of everyday existence. I was married, but was uneasy and fearful at even thinking about contentment, let alone going out and looking for it. I had a job, but it was factory work and it was dirty and menial, and although I hated it with a passion my fear of change, my fear of looking for something more fulfilling kept me with nose to the oily grindstone.

Many of the books I gathered promised answers. Within the bound pages (the cover blurb pledged) lay the happiness elixir that I so desperately sought. I would rush home from the bookshop (as I had rushed home from the bookshop many times before) sit down, tea in cup, book in hand, bum on seat, mind in the receptive mode and... disappointment. I did not find my truth!

Some of the books just plain lied. Some of them subtly withheld the truth. Others wouldn't have known the truth if it had fallen out of the sky and hit them on the head. And many more drew me into their literary parlour with tantalising promises, and then completely reneged on their pledge, leading me instead into a tangled, sticky web of moribund uncertainty.

In the end I got to thinking that perhaps there were no answers.

I felt that I had to do something if I was to make it through to the natural end of my incarnation without sinking deeper into the abyss or completely self-destructing. My mood was bible black, so giving up was often as close as my neck vein and (I have to tell you) sorely tempting, but I had my babies to consider and they needed me, so that selfish and self-pitying option was buried quick smart. Whilst I did not feel like a very competent father at that time, I did love my kids, and I was definitely unable to abandon them just to relieve my own pain. The other option was to vacate my dying existence and expand into a new reality, but it demanded testicles of hardened tungsten because every exit was guarded by a gargoyle of throbbing terror, a fear of failure, a fear of success, the fear of change, and the very real fear of no change at all... I figured that if I could face and embrace my dementors (by expanding out of my old orbit) my three-dimensional monsters would become two-dimensional cartoons.

As I said, there was a lot of fear in this option because I was scared of vacating a life that, whilst offensive to all my senses, was at least a devil I knew. But then I figured that my redundant incarnation was really no life at all, because in it I feared being mortal, and in it I was shrinking with every new calendar day. Like Reinhold Messner mid-point on his second failed ascent of the insurmountable and inhospitable Nanga Parbat, I was stuck halfway up my life, too scared to go any higher, too scared to go back down, too scared to stay where I was. In fact at one point – like Messner – I was actually too scared to live. And I cried for my life because it was not normal, and I so badly wanted to be normal again.

After one particularly bad depression, where the darkness nearly consumed me and where only my rock bottom broke the fall, I decided that if the mountain was not going to come to me, I was going to go to the mountain. I went out into the world of men without a compass or a map and I searched out my own answers in my own experiences, and I made sure that all of those experiences were brand new and challenging enough to add purchase to my attempt, a solid starting block, something that I could push against. And I also promised myself that once I found the answers that had thus far evaded me I would write them down in a book and get it into print. I made my vow with God to write down what I had found here and send it back as a gift to all those still left behind. And I would tell the whole truth and nothing but. I would not lie, I would not deceive and I would not make promises I could not keep.

So I went out and I experienced.

After climbing a pyramid of minor to major fears I reached my pinnacle nemesis: the fear of violent confrontation.

I did not like violent confrontation.

In fact, I didn't like confrontation of any description; if my then wife raised her matrimonial voice as much as one decibel and threatened cold dinners and a colder back in bed, whether the argument was on her side or not, I'd be on my begging knees pleading for reprieve, just to get things back to normal.

I liked things normal in those days, because normal felt safe. I later learned to eschew the norm because there is no growth in comfort; the terrorist in our lives is the reliving, day after day, what we already know, and where is the excitement in that? Where is the adventure? Where is the potential in rehashing life and reheating yesterday's leftovers?

At the time I was tall and skinny, in my late twenties and with a history of depression. My hair was receding and I had a tendency towards being easily offended (I didn't get out much!). I dared to be polite in an environment that saw gracious and read weak. I had three young children that I simply adored and a job for life at the factory that would make Prozac depressed.

These are not the credentials of a fighting man. I should not have been applying for work as a nightclub bouncer. Not by any normal standards. And I should definitely not have draped my skinny coil in a baggy tuxedo, nor gift wrapped my squeezy-bottle neck in a doorman's bow tie – and my bones should have been a million safe miles away from the cold pavement arena outside a city centre bar.

But happily I did apply, and I did get the job, and, yes, I was that baggy doorman leg-and-winged into a Saturday night frenzy of sharks and piranhas looking to displace a bad day or a bad life into a night of drunken violence. The next ten years were heady. I was bitten more times than a blind crocodile trainer but... I found the answers I was looking for regarding fear and its management. Now I had a story to tell. I had my experiences and, as promised, I wrote my book. I called it *Watch My Back* and in it I laid the truth bare.

That was a decade and a half ago and much has happened to me since, most of which I tell in the pages of my tome.

I can vividly remember the week it was published. How exciting.

I was still working as a (some felt) lowly doorman in the pubs and clubs of Coventry city centre. It was polled as the most violent city in Europe for its size and population and – partly inspired by this – Radio 1 wanted to interview me (me!) about my vast array of violent, funny, frightening, colourful and at times life-threatening experiences. At the time many thought I'd had a stroke of good luck getting the book into print – after all, I had no literary pedigree. That opinion neither impressed, swayed, nor mattered to me; all I cared about was the fact that I'd written a book, got it published and Radio 1 was coming to Coventry to do a feature on me.

This was 1992; I was working as a floor sweeper in an engineering factory by day, guarding people and doors and alcohol licences by night, and dreaming of one day, maybe, possibly, hopefully making my living as a full-time writer.

If most people were in agreement that I'd been lucky to get published, nearly everyone was unified in the belief that me becoming a full-time writer was as likely as my mum following Messner up Nanga Parbat in her carpet slippers and negligee.

More opinions that neither swayed nor mattered.

If I'd listen to majority opinion I would never have written the book in the first place. All I knew for definite was that, of all the books released in 1992 (and there were thousands), mine was the one that Radio 1 wanted to feature on their show.

Now, I am aware that violence was (always is) topical, and that a doorman writing a book (imagine!) was a novelty, and that perhaps not many people were taking me all that seriously. There were probably many arbitrary reasons for me being on Radio 1 but, again, none of them really mattered. What did matter was the fact that I had opened the door to a vast new reality, one that I was told did not exist for me and my likes, and now that it was open I had no intention of allowing it to close again. Not in this lifetime.

That Radio 1 feature showed me two very important things: 1) There was a greater interest in my book than was first assumed; 2) There was a massive potential to take my stories into radio, TV, film and audio. People tried to convince me that there was a limited, novelty value to my writing, and yet here I was being invited onto national talk shows with Hollywood superstars, whilst I was still working the doors. I even did an interview on Sky News live in front of millions of viewers.

For me, the highlight of the Radio 1 piece (with a lovely man called Mark Whittaker) was when they got an actor to dramatise a paragraph from *Watch My Back*. He read out a piece about me and John 'Awesome' Anderson; the incident was funny and violent and the actor read it beautifully and I remember listening and thinking, 'Wow – this book should be on audio.' It read so well; I was amazed at how the actor took the words, lifted them off the page and breathed three dimensions into them. I loved it. I promised myself that one day I would take this book – written in the field of action, with the naïve honesty and immediate clarity that is often lost in retrospect – and I would bring it to the big screen, and then I'd make it into an audio book, maybe even a TV series so that the stories, the lessons, the elixir of my experiences could be enjoyed and savoured and digested by all.

Of course, it took a little longer than I would have liked. I'd imagined in my contracted mind's eye that a large publisher would take the book off me and by the following year it would be on audio, on TV and at the pictures all at the same time. I didn't realise back then that book writing requires a high level of craft and a plethora of skills, many of which are learned and developed across a wide expanse of time and place. In my instance the writing apprenticeship has taken fifteen years, but my dream has now been realised. The 'local' book (and the local boy) that people thought might disappear in a season has been reincarnated in many forms – articles, books, short films, theatre, DVD – and now, a lifetime away from hearing it read for the first time on Radio 1, *Watch My Back* has made its way not only onto audio book, but also (at the same time) onto the big screen in a theatrical feature film called *Clubbed*.

If you had told me many years ago, when I was young and depressed, that one day my life story would be so full of colour that it would be in nine languages and that people would spend millions of pounds making it into a film, I might have called you a fantasist and accused you of giving this poor impressionable lad a lot of false hope. But of course, I was in a different place then. I was halfway up my inhospitable life, a life full of challenges and adversity that many people thought I might not overcome. But, like Messner on his third attempt at Nanga Parbat in 1970, I did reach the summit eventually, and I lived to tell the tale – oh, and I went onto climb many more mountains after that, of course. But that is another story, perhaps for another day.

Chapter 14

In the Room

Joan Rivers, the legendary American comedienne, was being interviewed for television by an aspiring comic, a young woman who held the stalwart in such high regard that her voice trembled into the microphone as she asked her questions.

It must have been very hard for you to make it in the world of stand up Miss Rivers, she said in all seriousness, *what with all the industry prejudice towards female performers. How did you ever get into the room?*

'The room' is aphoristic for being the elite in any specific field, in this case stand-up comedy. Everyone in every industry from hard-knock martial arts to high-end movie making is desperately trying to get into 'the room'.

Joan, not a lady to mince her words or mind her Fs and her Cs, replied to her interviewer (something along the lines of), *Don't be so fucking naïve! Being a woman has nothing to do with being in the room! If you've got the material you are in the room.*

Her reply momentarily stunned the interviewer, partly because it came at her like a Tyson hook, but mostly because the riposte took the legs out from under accepted belief. The young woman (and anyone else watching) was left clinging to the bullshit-ropes and in no doubt whatsoever that success cannot be hampered by gender (you cannot use that excuse any more!), only by lack of talent or, more probably, lack of intention. It is easier to blame your sex or your race or your colour or creed for a perceived failure than it is to say *I am not in the room because I am presently not good enough to be in the room.* If people keep prophesying (and believing in) prejudice and bias and any other pale excuse for not excelling then the chances are that they never will excel, because they are so busy looking for cop-outs, they forget to actually sit down and do the work.

I see the same infuriating, cloying naivety in all walks of life. People wanting to get into the room in martial arts, writing, art, industry. In fact, in any field you care to mention I can guarantee that it is teeming with people who call bias for blocking their entry to the room, when in fact the only thing that can ever block the doorway is the belief that there are forces at work to stop you other than yourself. So many people looking for an invitation – some of them solid people often with one foot already in the room – scupper themselves at the last minute by pointing a finger of blame and accusing *the powers* of discrimination when in fact the opposite is true.

There is no invite into the room; it is self-invite only.

Your bullshit keeps you out. Your *material* gets you in.

There is no protocol or chauvinism. No one cares about race or gender.

You are the only one that can get you in and you are the only one that can keep you out.

You are your own doorway; your talent (your fortune) is the key.

If you are not in the room, stop *looking out* for a reason and start *looking in*.

I see it in film all the time. Go onto any movie-making site on the Internet and scan the sorry diatribes (infected with invective) and see if I am not right; people bellyaching about how they are kept out of the room, the industry injustices, how very little help there is (out there) for the burgeoning talent, how heavily manned the entrance is and how greedy and precious its guards – as though anyone or anything could block their path if they produced the work.

Usually, the bleating sheep are those that are simply not industrious enough. They throw out a weekend script and then complain because Hollywood is not beating a path to their door.

We have a fellow (many fellows actually!) with a similar concern in Coventry – a martial artist, a nice man, a player but a player of some small repute. Sharon and I sat with him one day over a coffee whilst he lamented (we didn't stay long, lament is highly infectious and I didn't want to come down with it); he had trained for thirty years in the martial arts, he had the talent (he said) but he was not being allowed into the room. The martial elite were not letting him in. I was perplexed. Of course, I could see that he was not yet acclimatised enough to survive the room (the air is so thin), but I could see that he had the potential. Later I said to Sharon, 'This guy could do really well, why isn't he growing the talent to get him into the room?'

Sharon said something very profound, and it really helped me to understand not only the martial artist we'd just had coffee with, but also every other body (myself included) who wants to excel in any given area. She said, 'He is not developing the talent to take him into the room because he already thinks he has the talent to take him into the room, and that the current hierarchy are just not acknowledging it.'

How very true. He had overestimated his talent; because he thought he was already there (but that others could not or would not recognise it) he didn't feel he needed to do any more work. But, of course, he did need to do more work, a lot more. If he'd done enough, he would already be in the room! Full stop.

Entry is not policed by outside forces; it is automatic entry to those who have the material.

My friend thought he'd done the work because he had been training for thirty years, but in all honesty, knowing him as I do, he had been cruising probably for the last twenty. He was just not being honest with himself – you can't mistake time served for talent gained.

He was waiting for admittance instead of earning admittance.

And – as the old saying goes – if you're waiting, you're not working.

My advice is this: do the work, make your material so startlingly good that people will look *fucking* inadequate if they don't recognise you.

Then you won't be looking for the room. You'll be in the room, without even realising it. And people will be beating down your door for interviews and anecdotes and tips on how to make it. And when the young aspirant pokes a microphone under your nose (and he will) – looking for the secret ingredient whilst blaming the world for not proffering it, because of his age or her sex or the colour of their skin – and asks *how the hell did you get in the room with all those guards conspiring against the likes of us?* You'll be able to smile and use the immortal words of Queen Joan: *Don't be so fucking naïve...*

Next time you feel marginalised, and you feel as though *the man* is keeping you out of the room, remember, remember, remember: *If you've got the material, you're in the room.*

Chapter 15

Under the Bed
in a Biscuit Tin

I meditate every day. It enables me to connect with the Divine.

Twice a day actually.

Once in the morning before I start writing (at 5.30 a.m.) and once at night before retiring to bed (usually about 10.30 p.m.).

I like to do this for one reason and one reason alone: it is profitable.

I have realisations in my meditation that are shocking, revealing and often profound. I feel my consciousness expand with every thirty-minute investment. I find myself understanding more about myself and the cosmos around me than I do in normal waking consciousness. Some of this understanding I would like to share with you here.

But first a warning:

If meditation/prayer (I often pray in the meditative state) is so good for me (you might well ask) does that mean that more meditation is better?

I'd have to say that, for me personally, more is often not only *not better* but actually *worse*. You need to leave enough time in your day to live, to act, to roll up your sleeves and to help your wonderful life unfold.

Too much trance and not enough dance, as the saying goes, is not good for you.

Thirty minutes twice a day is plenty enough for me. I get everything I need from my two book-end sessions.

I have a few friends who use the meditative state excessively, but that is because they are scared to live. Like collecting certificates of educational achievement, but never leaving school. They use meditation as a hiding place. When life presents them with growing opportunities (difficulties) that need massive action and an investment of flesh-and-bone-and-sinew, they retreat to a small room (or even a different country) and slip (out of danger!) under a cerebral blanket of mantras and chakras and deep-state-consciousness (and denial), spending most of their time *out of time*. They often end up pale and un-lived, their minds brimming with wonder but their bones full of *wonder when the fuck are we going to actually do something?* Our minds do need a daily ration of quiet, of that there can be no doubt, but equally our bodies long to taste the cold steel of corporeal existence.

Back to the shocking, revealing and downright profound.

You pretty much receive daily revelations when you are a practiced meditator, too many for one small article, so I will share three that stand out.

My first shocking revelation came after half a lifetime of blaming God for abandoning me when I was a child. I didn't realise that I was blaming God, not initially. It only came to light during a particularly difficult purification period, when I was coming to terms with the fact that someone fucked my head by sexually invading my body when I was 12 years old. I was aware that the incident had been a violation of my impressionable youth, and I understood that it had given birth to what is known in psychology as an abandonment schema, where a traumatic incident triggers a (false) belief that no one can ever be trusted and that everyone, especially those that should not, eventually will abandon you. I was also painfully aware that this historical schema was causing me current agony, because I was experiencing lots of paranoia and psychotic sexual jealousy in my relationships. Also – as a physical defence against possible further assaults – I had developed an intolerant and violent alter-ego, one that literally stamped the head of any threat into the pavement like a squashed bug.

This behaviour was causing me untold problems and – as a method of clearing this menacing, if not well-meaning shadow – I had started to practice deep meditation. It was during one such heightened state that I spoke with God. I found myself becoming very angry, and asking the Big Man, 'So, tell me, why the fuck did you abandon me when I needed you most? I was twelve!'

For a long second there was quiet. Then a benevolent voice, one that I did not recognise as my own. It said, 'I didn't abandon you.'

A pause while I took this information in and digested it. And then the voice asked *me* a question, 'Did you abandon you?'

Did I abandon me? That is what He asked. And that was the first time I realised that I had not been abandoned by God. I don't think that I abandoned myself either. I believe that, as a consequence of the trauma I underwent, an outgrowth was born. I (my younger self) stopped developing the very night of my attack. As though the sheer terror of what I underwent froze me in time. A newer, braver me, a *warrior self* carried my young bones safely out of that dark night, and into adulthood. He acted as shield and armour to my adolescent self. I feel this to be true because my 12-year-old self was still residing somewhere inside me, in a repressed pouch, some warm, hidden unconscious pocket. He came forward, terrified, and made himself known every time life placed me in a relationship that might lead to further abandonment. Future pain. Potential terror.

But a terrified and blind 12-year-old is a dangerous entity when you keep him inside the body of a grown man who has developed the physical skills to kill people. The old me was creating havoc inside the new me, and lots of people in the world of men were getting savaged (and ravaged) because of it (read *Watch My Back*). So, reluctantly but gratefully I had to let *Geoff the younger* go. That early conversation with God, where He showed me that I had not been abandoned, was the first stage in this process – acknowledging that God had not let me down, recognising that someone inside me was stuck and needed release (and that he was desperately sad but frighteningly dangerous). And understanding that now was the time to let him go changed me forever.

Over the next few years, through a little prayer and meditation, and a lot of work in the physical world, I was gradually able to release my pain and free myself from the torment of jealousy and fear and violence. The revelation was an inside job. The release came from acting on the new information in the world of men. What had been revealed was amazing, but impotent without the purifying addition of hard labour.

A very revealing insight came to me when I was trying to expand my business. For a long time my wife

Sharon and I had run a company selling inspiration to the masses, and we had experienced much success. But for the last few years we seemed to have stalled. The business was no longer growing and I couldn't understand why. Having always believed that the self is the source of all problems and the hub for every solution, I went into a meditation to try to find the answer. If my business was not growing because of me I wanted to know why, so that I could dissolve the issue and move on. I quickly realised through deep introspection that I had an issue with money, or should I say I had an issue with having a lot of money. Being brought up in a working-class family where cash was always sparse, and where both of my parents had to work long hours just to get by, I had developed very negative associations with having money. I had lots of experience of fiscal need, but none at all with monetary abundance.

In the Upanishads there is a beautiful verse that says, 'They took abundance from abundance, and abundance still remained.' Whilst I innately believed in universal abundance, I had no actual experience or proof of that profusion. My reality was one of lack, where *money does not grow on trees*, where there was *never enough to go around,* and asking for more always equated to being greedy and selfish. This was what I marinated in for thirty years. It was not just a part of what I believed – it was my whole belief system.

The words that stuck in my head most were *greedy* and *selfish*. I believed that asking for more money and having more money was a greedy and selfish thing to do. And don't even get me started on my Catholic upbringing, where I was not only told on a daily basis that money was the source of all evil, but also that if I ever did become a rich man I had as much chance of getting to heaven as I did of squeezing my camel through the eye of a needle.

So I meditated on it.

Was it greedy to want/hope/pray for more? And in a deep meditation I found myself in space, travelling, surrounded by stars and galaxies. I was actually there. This was no dream, I was awake, eyes closed (no drugs, honest!) but surrounded by constellations.

Then that voice again.

The benevolent One.

It asked me to observe the stars in the sky.

There were billions and billions of stars.

I observed.

'All of those stars,' said the voice, 'were created by the desires of man. They are the creation of man's imagination. The universe,' it went on, 'is expanding. And it is expanding because of your creation. Asking for more is not greedy or selfish. Asking for more, desiring more, creating more, is simply playing your role in creation. So ask for as much as you want. You are not being greedy, you are being creative.'

This made a lot of sense to me. It resonated deep inside.

But I still had this niggling doubt, this feeling that I was greedy and selfish. I had probably heard the phrase ten thousand times as I was growing up, so it was hard to exorcise. Sensing my qualm, the Voice said something else, something that was more revealing still. It said, 'You think that you are worried about greed and selfishness, but you are not. Actually, what you are really afraid of is greed and selfishness.'

Excuse me?

Isn't that what I just said? This made no sense.

The voice continued.

'You do not fear that *wanting* more is greedy and selfish, you fear that *having* more will make you become greedy and selfish. You are afraid of having money, in case you cannot control the power of having money. Money is not the root of all evil; it is the misuse of money that has evil at its root.'

Wow! That was not only revealing, it was also very true.

I was worried that if I had lots of money and a bigger business I might become irresponsible, one of those selfish greedy people that are afraid to share their spoils, and hide their wealth under the bed in a biscuit tin. Money, I was informed, was a good provider, and for those that volunteered to be the caretaker of much wealth there came great responsibility. Like a tree that takes abundance from the earth and holds that abundance in its roots, and in its trunk and in its branches (its infrastructure for serving), you have to develop leaves and fruit as a way of distributing it all back into the abundance it came from.

Those that were powerful acted as a God-given conduit for wealth. Those that failed to get through the eye were the ones that made the naïve mistake of thinking that they owned the abundance, and so tried to horde and hide it.

I knew from experience that these traits I feared (greed and selfishness) were healthy fears; knowing that power can corrupt (and absolute power can corrupt absolutely) and being aware of the corruptive nature of money was not a forewarning as much as it was a forearming. Becoming selfish and greedy was not a lottery, it was a choice. If I chose and intended to be neither, then I would become neither. And having more money, creating more stars, expanding my own universe and the universe around me, would be a body-building exercise for my character. And – of course – hitting that fiscal peak would also give me a greater perspective to future goals. It is easier to see God from a Rolls Royce, as the guru Osho once said.

One of the very profound revelations that came to me came to me very recently.

Like the great inventor and philanthropist Buckminster Fuller, I discovered (close to my fiftieth year) that altruism is not only a worthy endeavour, it is also a highly profitable one. When Mr Fuller reached the age of forty, he looked back and took an inventory of his life thus far and (in his own words) it had not been impressive. He had been largely unsuccessful in life and in business and he wanted to assess why. Looking back with a self-honesty that was both rare and inspirational he discovered a life-altering profundity; all of the unsuccessful events in his life came after he tried to achieve something purely for his own benefit, and all of his (accidental) triumphs were the direct result of being spontaneously altruistic, outrageously generous. In other words, when he did things that benefited others more than himself he was massively successful. When he thought only of serving himself he failed more often than he succeeded, and if he succeeded the success was nothing you could really shake a stick at.

Thinking only of himself, he realised, was thinking very small.

But when he thought of serving others, especially when he thought of serving a multitude of others, he started to think big, big, big.

On realisation of this, Buckminster (for beautifully selfish reasons) decided from there on in to only create things that would serve millions and millions of people. He knew that the more people he intended to serve, the bigger his thinking would become, and subsequently the grander his success. And over his lifetime this proved to be magnificently true. He became an amazing, global phenomenon.

So, I too realised from my own experiences that altruistic thinking was big thinking. And that whilst I thought only of myself, my thinking and my creation would always stay very local. As a consequence, in my meditation I stopped asking God to serve me; I ceased from saying *show me how to better serve myself*, and instead asked, 'Lord, how I might serve You?' My thinking was simple enough; if I served God, who is omniscient, omnipotent and omnipresent, then I would serve absolutely and unequivocally everyone. And in that everyone (of course) I include myself. My focus of prayer and meditation every morning and every night became thus: 'Lord, show me how to serve You. I will to will Thy will. Place me where I can serve You better.' Suddenly my thinking got bigger, my creation grander and my opportunities wider reaching. I was getting phone calls and emails and letters from people from across the globe who desperately wanted to help me get my work out to more people, who desperately wanted to help me get *me* out to more people. The results were staggering (since beginning this method of asking I discovered that my book *Watch My Back* has been Googled over three million times!). And the only change I made was to ask in my meditation to serve God. This was profound enough, but it was not the most profound thing that happened. The most profound thing that happened (and I must tell you about this immediately because it is so exciting) happened very recently. I was meditating and, as usual, I asked God (as l always ask God) to 'show me how to serve You. I will to will Thy will. Place me, Lord, where you want me Lord.' Nothing unusual so far. The words were the same. My mantra was identical to the one I had used for as long as I could remember. Only something very profound changed this day. Something was different. It was not the words, rather it was the direction of the words that staggered me. I realised immediately that this time it was not me saying, 'Let me serve you God.' It was God saying, 'Let Me serve you.' It was not me stating, 'I will to will Thy will,' it was the Will, saying to me, 'I will to will thy will.' He was saying 'Geoff, what do you want? Where do you want me? How can I serve you? What do you want to experience? How can I help you to do that? I will to will thy will.'

I was suddenly very aware that the prayer was not going *in* to God, the prayer was coming *out* from God. It was not me asking God to serve Him, it was

God asking me, to serve me. It was very clear at that moment; I was living a corporeal existence, like a kid at school, and God was teaching through me, and He wanted to teach me whatever I wanted to learn. All I had to do was ask. All this time I was waiting for God's command, thinking, 'Soon I'll get a sign,' when all the time God was patiently waiting for me to ask for direction, he was looking to me for a sign, so that He could give me the sign I was waiting for.

Shocking, revealing and very profound all in one, I am sure you will agree.

No need to be greedy, it all belongs to us. No need to search for revelations, we are the revelation, we just have to sit still for long enough and be quiet for long enough to realise that we are not just in the field of diamonds, we are the field of diamonds. And if you want profundity, you need do no more than look in the mirror and be pleased by the miracle that stares back at you.

The vault, the key and the treasure inside are all looking right back at you.

Chapter 16

The Many-failed Soul

I like critics, those many-failed souls.

I love them.

Especially the nasty ones.

I really like, really love, simply adore the fellow or the lass that sits behind a desk or a computer and types their destruction of a soul (or a soul's work) for the world to gorge on (how proud their parents must be).

Recently I have released my first feature film, *Clubbed*, into the cinemas and we had very mixed reviews, a polarity that ranges from the very dire 'worst film of the year' to the wonderful and uplifting 'the new Clockwork Orange!' Some of the polarity actually came from different people within the same newspaper: *The Sun* called it 'the new Trainspotting' and its sister paper the *News of the World* gave it one star. *The Times* also gave us one star, whilst the *Sunday Times* said, 'British film has never been so good.'

It's apparent that the 'powers' cannot even agree amongst themselves, so in my eyes this deems their critique worthless. You cannot take criticism seriously when it comes from someone that uses his left hand to stab his right arm.

But I do love them because whatever they say, whatever they do, they will not and they cannot hurt me.

Their vitriol, their savage disregard, their heartlessness disenchants them, it disembowels them (their innards on show for all to see) and it belittles them.

But their words cannot faze me. Their words can arm me. They can weather me.

They can instruct me. They definitely (thank you very much) can temper me.

But they can never destroy me because I am surrounded by God. I am drenched in light. I am not as hard as nails (as some might suppose), I am soft and I am yielding. And as we all should know, when two forces meet, the one who is able to yield will conquer.

But here is the main gist of this story: if I am to be protected from the negative critique, then I also need to eschew the good reviews (of which we had many) because they are just as insidious, and just as individual. What this recent episode has taught me is that as long as I like what I do, and as long as I have faith in my work and integrity, then whatever others might think, good or bad, will neither lift me nor dash me down.

If you have equanimity, then all reviews are good.

Chapter 17

Kissing Lepers

When you get a minute – today... *now* preferably – I want you to do me a favour. I want you to go out, into the street, into the town, the city or the fields and find yourself a leper. Introduce yourself first, it is only proper, but as soon as the formalities are over and hands have been shaken I want you to hold that lovely leper in a warm embrace and kiss him or her on the lips.

Yes, you heard me right!

Kiss that leper (I can feel a game show coming on) fully on the lips. If they are cracked and bleeding, if their flesh is ravaged and torn and dismembered body parts litter their path, and if the cold shiver of repulsion marks your spine as a rabbit run, good. Good, good, good. The more terror the better. It means that you have found the right leper.

Kiss the leper.

Hug the leper.

Embrace the leper and wrap that beautiful disease up into a coat of wool and warmth. Carry them up into your arms and deliver their flayed skin and protruding bones to the nearest care, because that leper is a part of the *hidden you* and they are begging for respite.

Now, I am not naïve and I can already intuit your thoughts. The words forming on your lips are also as obvious as they are expected – and the excuses shaping your escape route are not bespoke; they are my excuses, they are the excuses of every person. Not only are you thinking *this guy has had his marbles sucked out with an industrial vacuum-cleaner*, but you are also thinking *lepers are not as easy to come by as they once were!*

It is true. They no longer wander city and street, with neither love nor home, ringing their bell of despair, neither do they solicit quite the level of repulse once apportioned to them; the disease has found some cure, and the diseased a flash of hope, so the fear of contagion has been managed somewhat.

But you have probably figured out by now that my use of the darling leper is allegorical, and *I know* that *you will know* that the leper I am really talking about is not such a rarity; he is in fact en masse in our cities and streets, he is *the abundant* pouring from

99

abundance, not only in the world of men, but also into the very bones of you and me.

The leper is called fear.

My next suggestion, whilst not nearly as demonstrative or oblique as the first, should still proffer an equal gush of trepidation. At least I hope.

I want you to go out (or go in) and find your own leper and kiss them on the lips, and in doing so kiss them a fairly goodbye.

St Francis of Assisi, a man both historically and universally admired for his brutal life of asceticism and service, spent his entire life on this spinning rock chasing, confronting and dissolving the shadows that lay between himself and the light of God. Anything that frightened him, anything that seduced him and anything that repulsed him he walked towards, he confronted and he overcame. Not always willingly or even courageously – often his confrontation with demons was reluctant, and more often still, he entered the fiery brimstone night in a state of abject terror.

But he did enter, and he kept entering until his heavy coat of black had been finally shed.

In the time of Francis and in the district of Assisi, leprosy was still a growing curse, and the sound of the leper's bell was as familiar as it was terrifying. Certainly for our erstwhile saint who had an unnatural and powerful aversion to these poor, diseased souls. Ascending this terror-mountain (at the command of God) proved to be the pivotal moment on this beautiful man's journey through life.

The story goes thus: already on his way to sainthood, Francis confided in a friend that, whilst he tirelessly embraced the heroic life, there was still one fear he could not overcome. Although he despised himself for such an un-Christian hate, he felt nauseous at the mere ring of a leper's bell.

Of course, as we all should know, a fear spoken is a shadow brought into the light.

And we always attract the things we fear.

The very night after Francis spoke his fear aloud he heard the command of God: *Francis, I want you to go out, I want you to find a leper and I want you to kiss him on the lips and embrace him.*

Now, being Francis of Assisi – sainted stoic, revered monk – you would probably expect him to hear the call of God and start his search, without argument and without err.

Not so.

Francis was many great things and his was a laudable existence, but above and beyond all he was a man with all the associated limitations and weaknesses that being flesh-bound brought – and I think this is what I love about him more than anything else.

He did exactly what you and I would do if asked to embrace our greatest fear; he protested, he complained, he cried – he even accused God of torturing him. When he asked God, 'Why do you punish me?' God said simply, 'Because I love you.'

Once Francis realised that God's command was really God's love, he ecstatically raced towards the very first leper he happened upon, grabbed the startled soul, embraced him like a beloved and kissed his cracked and bleeding lips. He then wrapped a cloak around the walking infection and began carrying him 'skin and bone' to the nearest colony.

Francis had not walked very far before he noticed that the leper he was carrying had grown light. He stopped to investigate, opened the cloak and, to his amazement, the leper was no longer there. He had disappeared. It was at this moment that Francis realised, properly realised, what God was trying to show him: that all fear was phantom, that it had no existence outside of mind, and that a leper kissed and lovingly embraced would dissolve into mist. The reason this proved to be such a monumental experience for Francis, and a turning point in his legendary life, was because it became a powerful reference point. When God brought him greater challenges in the future and doubt came to the fore, he always remembered the leper, how heavy and fearful he had appeared in the eye of anticipation and yet how beautiful he became when kissed, and light when carried.

He understood that all fears are constructs of imagination, lepers in the eye of mind. In fully realising and accepting this he was able to dissolve every fear and thus grow closer to Unity, nearer to God.

So... when you get a minute – today... now preferably – I want you to do *yourself* a huge favour; that leper who has been haunting you for so long, the one standing between you and your dreams, you and your freedom, go out, grab him, kiss him, embrace him too hard and with too much love and with as much haste as you can muster and don't be at all surprised when, on lifting him, he vanishes like the morning mist.

This leper's bell does not sound a forewarning to the frightened; it rings out a call to the brave.

Chapter 18

Participating Anthropic Principle

Forty-eight years of hanging from this blue marble gambolling through space has taught me much, most of which is so anti-intuitive that people turn a deaf ear when I proffer my fortune (free of charge!).

But I will keep trying to impart this sapient ware because I need to serve in order that I might make room for more, and I do intend to know more.

So I try again – offering my lessons to you, whoever you might be.

Lesson One – Wealth
It is easy to think (intuitive to think) that the more we keep the wealthier we will become, so we tend

to cut our costs, place our fortune under the bed in a biscuit tin and make our creditors chase for payment – and in doing so we call ourselves savvy! We become masters of profit and loss, speculation and accumulation, assets and liabilities. We tighten our belts, we give nothing away unless we feel it is a loss leader, or that it might buy us a favour in the fiscal arena.

What I have learned contravenes this given law. The more I give away freely, with thought of service but not of profit, the richer I seem to get. Generous gifting of love, time and materials confirms my belief in abundance, and so abundance more than I could ever imagine fills and expands the void left by my philanthropy. Like a muscle spent, my given wealth expands more with every giving. The Bible confirms my finding, as do the Gita and the Upanishads and every other tome of great historical and religious significance.

But it is my experience that offers the greatest proof.

So I continue to give. And give.

Never pulling another's cart, because that would be a disservice; every child deserves the chance to suffer deliberately at the yoke and grow. Instead I assist those who work their limit and need only a word or a smile or a doff of the hat to help them spill over the tipping point into success.

Lesson Two – Humility

When I praise others and help them shine I myself shine like polished brass. I spent duller and duller years trying to make myself glow only to find a dust enveloping me like a grey sweater. By accident I once reversed my (unsuccessful) technique and quite genuinely gave praise to another over myself and whilst he was buffered to a gleam by all, more shine still found its way back to me.

So I started to make it a practice, I married myself to authentic humility and showered praise where it was warranted at every and any opportunity, and the gods beat a shimmering path to my door and begged to buff my boots to a glow.

Lesson Three – Creativity

When I think and say and act from my core I create humour and profundity and couture. People say *your work is so funny, your work is profound – it is so original.* So next time, fired by their enthusiasm, I double my efforts; I dig very deep to mine for the laughs, the depth and the bespoke. However, all my efforts bring forth are the cliché, the ephemeral and the antique.

I have learned that who I am and what I do is enough and, if I relax and flow and stop forcing, the good stuff will deliver itself in exactly the right format and at exactly the right time.

You cannot order brilliance, you can only deliver it.

Lesson Four – Looking for Diamonds

I always innately knew that I was standing in the middle of a field of diamonds, but my unschooled eyes saw only glass and my blind fingers found only rocks. And my frustration only dulled my seeing more and left my hands fat and clumsy at the search. I ran around the field fervidly but found nothing of value other than the knowledge that fervent searching does not lead to finding. So I quelled my zeal, slowed my heart and stopped. I sat. I sat very still and long, until my brass-band mind stopped clashing symbols and beating drums and the instruments were put away.

I stopped searching for *profit diamonds* and I found a crystal quiet.

And then very gradually, in my muted state, a diamond appeared on the periphery.

I didn't find it, it found me.

Then another diamond. And another and another and another until I could not see my field for sparkling gems, so many that I could not collect them all in a galaxy of lifetimes.

Lesson Five – Power!

I wanted power. So I did the thing that I thought might bring me power; I lifted weights... but the power that I gained was temporary and incomplete. So I placed on my armour – muscle, tattoos, aggression-masks and information about how to maim and kill – and I went into battle with life. But the power of muscle and the technique of the kill were limited and limiting and like a boomerang what I used to attack returned to me in an arc of violence. So I went, instead, for wealth and built myself a fiscal castle, where the walls were made of gold and the turrets were cast from silver and the gates were made from oak and brass and precious stone. But the bejewelled bastion that impressed the world of men lost its worth with me because its power was brought and temporal.

So I sat down and stopped trying to be powerful.

I accessed God, the authentic Power, and He laughed from the heavens at my efforts thus far and He said to me *stop trying to be powerful, just try to Be.*

So I expanded into His power until I united with the 'I Am' and suddenly I found access to the whole cosmos and I understood at once that ours is a man-centred universe – man is God – and that if I engaged the Participating Anthropic Principle (to seek softly, but with expectation of finding) and intended it, not only would mountains move and seas part but I could create a supernova simply by looking to the night skies and expecting to see one.

Power is not in being simply strong. Power is simply in being.

Chapter 19

I Am My Only Enemy, I Am My Only Friend

I think God wants us to grow. I believe that the universe is hungry for us to expand – and it is continually offering us the means to accomplish this. Many people feel that meditation is the prime exercise for this expansion, and whilst I agree that it is hugely beneficial, I have to add my own personal experience-based caveat; whilst I love to expand my conscious net though meditation, I have to say that my very deep development always came (and continues to come) through my very hard experience where I learn to dissolve fear whilst facing fear, and expand into new realities by engaging new realities. An example: I nearly killed a man once in a car park match-fight. Afterwards I saw God. It was the last place I expected to encounter Him, but He was there and he spoke to me through my fear and my pain. I was certain that this man (my opponent) was dead and I was also certain that my life was over. After a bloody encounter (triggered by two obese egos and an argument over personal territory) he was deeply unconscious and on his way to hospital and I was in my own version of Dante's inferno. Within minutes of the affray I was deeply remorseful, within hours I believed I was on my way to prison. When I drove my car home that night – it was about midnight – I felt as though my world had collapsed. If he was dead, and I was sure he was, I was about to lose everything that I held dear; ironically everything I had become complacent of. It was then that the realisation hit me: I was about to lose the most precious gift of all. My liberty. My car seemed to be flying, the roads glimmered like gold, the street lights were glowing, celestial orbs. When I got home my wife was asleep in one room, my children in another, completely unaware of my crime and my pain. As I lay next to my wife on the bed she seemed so much more beautiful than the lady I had left to go to work just six hours earlier. She was positively glowing. Her skin was like silk, it was as though the corporeal veil had dropped and I could see right into her soul. My kids appeared to me like angels, I just could not believe how beautiful they were – and I was about to lose them all.

Then another startling realisation; the man I kicked around the tarmac like a football, the man that I had dehumanised, the man I had thought my enemy, was also a human being, someone's husband, someone's father, someone's son. I was filled with remorse. I unashamedly got onto my knees and prayed to God, I asked Him for one more chance, I promised that if He allowed this man to live I would turn this baby around, I would change my life. After a very long dark night of the soul I found out that the guy had not only survived, he was actually walking around completely without injury. I kept my promise, I renounced violence and I started my search for meaning. The huge revelation for me here, which was epiphanic, was that all those folk I felt were my enemies were not my enemies; I have no enemies. I am my only enemy, I am my only friend.

Another experience-based epiphany occurred when I delved heavily into the martial aspect of the combat arts and learned how to kill people. You would think that if you trained intently in a killing art that it would give you a thirst for killing, but the opposite is true; the ability to kill, taking the martial arts to its obvious ends, triggered a transition in me. I could feel how ugly it was to hurt another person, and suddenly all I wanted to do was hug everyone. Of course, at the time I had a reputation for being a fighting man, so everyone thought that my marbles and I had parted company, but I was actually happier than I had ever been; all I wanted to do was help people, serve people, and the thought of harming another human being was anathema to me. These revelations might seem obvious; you will have read about the futility of violence many times, I am sure. You will have read about killing all your enemies by making them friends, no doubt. But for me this was not mere information taken from a library or a book of quotes, it was not learned, this was earned wisdom, it was actual elixir. I can now say with certainty that violence always rebounds on itself, and I can use this knowledge to take all violence out of my life. I can say with absolute faith that I have no enemies and pray even (and especially) for those that would do me harm. This is what extreme physical experience gave me. I have had similar thoughts and revelations in meditation, but until I tested them, they remained simply pregnant pieces of information looking for a birth in the outside world.

But of course, I was always up for a physical challenge because I wanted to be free. As much as I love meditation and as much as I practice it and concur on its benefits, I do find that people are often guilty of courting deep states of relaxation in order to avoid raw states of experiential growth. I was never a man to sit at a bar and talk challenge, or theorise challenge or intellectualise challenge. I didn't take the concept of challenge to a lab and do qualitative and quantitative experiments with mice or rats. I took my bones out onto the concrete; I was my own experiment. I was 'Rat A' and the world was my laboratory. If it worked I got to walk away. If it didn't I ended up in a police cell or a hospital ward. Ironically, what I found was that all the external challenges I faced as a martial artist, and as a nightclub doorman and as a man in the world of men, turned out to be internal challenges, they all forced me back inside. The real jihad was the internal jihad. In fact, all jihads are battles with the self. But for me it was only in facing the fears and challenges that I had created out there – because ultimately they are only projections from the self, or maya (illusion) – that I was able to level the hills and fill the valleys 'in here'. The bigger challenges are often closer than you think. It is easier to march angrily through London with an 'anti-war' banner than it is to pick up the phone and end the war with the sister that you don't talk to anymore, the ex-wife that hates your guts or the son/daughter that you haven't seen since that family argument all those lost years ago. People want to stop the war 'out there' whilst the war in their own life, or inside their own bodies, is raging away almost unnoticed and often ignored. I think that 'out there' is often an easy distraction for what is inside. People are in love with the idea of challenge but do not actually take on the real challenge; they want to change the world but are unable to even change their own personal habits. They want sovereignty over the material before earning sovereignty over the self. Idyllic retreats and lonely caves are nice and I highly recommend them for respite and recovery and for the odd sojourn, but they do not prepare you for the world of men. The world of men is where you prepare for the world of men. With that thought as my sponsor I changed my whole universe for the better. And my method was simple; I made a list of all the things that I dreamed of doing, all the things that I was frightened of doing... and I did them. But in order to do that I had one major hurdle to overcome. Myself. I was my own enemy. So I killed my enemy by making him my friend. If you want to master the world, first master yourself. If you want to take on the world, start first by taking on the self.

Chapter 20

Slings and Arrows

I have always attracted a bit of criticism, with my maverick martial arts and my very honest writing, but I went through a phase recently where I was getting more than usual. People were slinging stones of insult at my back, and firing arrows of vitriol – on the Internet and in the newspapers.

I was perplexed.

Why were people slinging stones and firing arrows at my back?

Then it occurred to me (and I smiled, delighted).

They are slinging and firing at my back because I am moving away from them at a pace. They do not make queues to tell me to my face, let me tell you.

I was moving like a fast thing through the narrow gate (it was a tight squeeze, but I got through) and into a brand new orbit, *the new world*.

The stones are still being slung, the arrows are still firing, but now they are hitting air.

And now they fall short behind me. Now they are gone.

When you expand into new orbits the jealous and the profane always sling stones and they always fire arrows. And it is always at your back.

It is a good sign. A sign that you are on the right path.

Pioneers always get attacked (it's in the job description).

It is how they know that they are pioneers.

Chapter 21

Ten Thousand Angels

Do you fancy a walk on water? How about moving a mountain at command, or parting waves with the flick of a Moses hand?

Nothing is impossible if you have faith. But to gain faith one has to eschew doubt.

How do we do that?

In the face of outrageous pessimism how do we vanish the horned shadow of qualm?

If you understand your holy inheritance, you, like me, can call upon the power of ten thousand angels and your doubt will squirm behind you like a cowering Satan.

I love the story in the Bible about Jesus of Nazareth and the disciple Peter, when they walked on water. It is a great example of faith.

I love it for several reasons, not least that I do worship Jesus Christ.

Some people think that the story is parabolic or a fancy allegory or an imaginary figment of some historical imagination. I choose to believe that it is one of the true miracles of Christ, and my faith in that legend is important to me.

The story goes thus:

Peter and the disciples of Jesus Christ are on a ship out at sea. This was when they were still men of the world, casting nets for a fishy catch, before they became fishers of men. On this occasion the sea – as it is prone to do in biblical lore – took a stormy turn for the worse and started tossing the ship like a piece of balsa. The waves were raging and the disciples feared for their very lives. But the fear of the *contrary sea* was nothing next to the terror they felt when across the tumultuous waves strolled Jesus of Nazareth, as casual as you or I on our Sunday amble.

He was walking on the water.

The men were terrified and thought Jesus a spirit, and when he spoke to them in their terror it doubled. When Jesus saw their fright he begged them, 'Fear not, it is I, Jesus.' He tried to reassure them that he was no spirit, but they were not convinced.

'If it is really you Jesus,' a doubting Peter said, 'then bid me to walk beside you on the water.' So Jesus bid him out from the boat and Peter – filled with faith

– was able to walk on the sea too. But as he walked across the waves towards Jesus and he saw the rage of the water beneath his feet and all around him Peter suddenly erred. A second of doubt became a crippling loss of faith and he quickly started to sink into the ocean. He cried out, 'Save me Jesus, save me.' Jesus held out his hand and lifted Peter out of the water and said, 'You of little faith, why did you doubt?'

Faith had enabled Peter to walk on water. Lack of faith saw him sinking faster than the UK pound against the US dollar as I write.

When he asked Jesus for help, Peter called upon the power of ten thousand angels.

We can all do this, any time we want. We can all close our eyes and ask our God to help us, to guide us and when necessary to save us.

I ask for help every single day.

The two men returned to the ship, where the storm suddenly and miraculously calmed.

What I love about this story is what it represents to me. Whether you believe in Jesus Christ or miracles is of little consequence – what is important is that you see the literal meaning of this story. To me, the ship that the disciples find themselves on represents the world of comfort and safety; the known. Your safe, comfortable world, your job, your house, your religion, your relationships, your caste and your beliefs. It represents what you know. The stormy water, of course, that galaxy of salty wet, represents discomfort, the dangerous unknown, the big world out there.

And Jesus walking on the water represents the seemingly impossible.

And let us be in no doubt of one thing: the impossible is never really impossible, it is just an opportunity that we have yet to find a solution for.

Jesus himself in the story represents faith.

And what Jesus is saying is: *I am doing something that you believe is impossible to prove to you: the possibility of the impossible.*

When Peter has faith he walks on water, the same as Jesus; when he allows doubt to enter into his mind he starts to sink. It is his faith that creates the miracle and his lack of faith that makes impossibility out of the possible.

For Peter to achieve his miracle (in this case to walk on water) he has to leave the safety of the known, the safety of the ship, and step out into the unfamiliar (or the frightening). Jesus is acting as a man of congruence, he is saying: *I can do it, I am showing you that it can be done, now you do it.* By walking on water he demonstrates the miracle in order to make it possible for all. He is the embodiment of his message, he is his own gospel. He is not just saying *it can be done* and simply expecting you to believe, he is showing that it can be done so that believing is easier.

I re-read the story of Jesus walking on water again yesterday. I like to revisit the miracles periodically. I find them to be an inspirational reminder of my heritage. Especially in these so-called recessionary times. The first thing I did after I closed the Bible was look at my own life, my own beliefs, my own safe boats and my own impossible dreams. And I reassessed them. And whilst I don't plan to make a literal attempt at walking on the sea any time soon (all in good time, my friends, all in good time), I definitely and unequivocally am going to break my comfort zones and reclassify my list of impossible things. And more than anything else I am going to ask for more faith so that, even if water walking and mountain moving and the parting of large expanses of sea are not at the top of my to-do list, all those other impossible dreams will be. Because... nothing is impossible if you have faith!

Faith is charged with the power of ten thousand biblical angels, and if we call upon the ten thousand, mountains and seas and water walk-ways will be very small pickings, my friends; even the stars and the constellations will quiver before our might.

Chapter 22

Gospel

When you smoke your cigarettes – even if you think they don't see – you are teaching the kids to smoke cigarettes.

Do not doubt me on this. It is fact. And your lesson is an assault; it is an abuse on young bodies and malleable minds.

You can educate yourself and your children by reading books on law and morality but it will not compensate because your gospel is what you do and not what you say. Words without action will simply bounce off the windscreen of young minds.

It is how you live that counts.

When you deal in deception – even if you think the kids don't see you deal in deception – when you fiddle your taxes, when you buy your bent gear (when you steal, in other words) when you lie (even if it is just a little white lie) and when you fail to tell the truth (which is simply another way of dealing in lies) you teach your kids the art of deception.

Do not doubt me on this. It is fact. And your lesson is disabling; it is a virus on the hard drive of soft young minds.

You can evangelise until the second coming about honesty and integrity and about doing the right thing, you can quote from holy scroll and preach from church pulpit, but your words will be vaporised by the acid of wrong action because your gospel is what you do and not what you say.

Words without action are impotent. It is how you live that counts.

When you are violent – even if you think the kids do not see you dealing in violence – you are schooling the kids in the art of violence.

Do not doubt me on this. It is fact. And your tutorial is an abomination, a savage, slashing impression left in the psyche of young minds. Violence is a demon intent that employs thoughts, looks, words as well as deeds as its weapons of war. And you can shake your fist at the sky all day long, condemning the school bully, the street hoodie and the government warmongers and the wrongs they inflict upon the world but none of it will even reach young minds, and none of it will instruct because your gospel is always, always, always what you do and never (never, never) what you say. Because words without action are like wheels without traction.

It is how you live that counts.

Teaching children is easy enough in principle, but very hard to place into action. If you want them to live a clean life, live a clean and splendid life yourself. Everything else is the folly of foolish and ignorant denial.

As Saint Francis of Assisi said, we should all preach the gospel, and if we really need to, we should use words.

So why not preach an amazing gospel, why not live clean, be honest, eschew violent ways and achieve your own very best potential by living the dream you dare to tell them they can live? That way you need never open your mouth to prophesise, because one solitary inspirational action will speak louder than a library of good advice.

Chapter 23

Buccaneering Rabbits

Depression is a funny old thing; when you are in it you feel as though you are never going to escape, and when you finally do get out you feel as though you could never be depressed again.

But in the back of your mind you nurture that quiet dread; will it return again and drag my bones into that dark abyss?

This is where I found myself in the early eighties, depressed (for no clear reason, other than the fact that my creative aspirations were not being met by my current reality), scared and thoroughly despondent. My hopelessness came not just from being depressed (again – I had a history) but rather from the fear that, if I didn't do something soon to combat my manic attacks, depression might end up becoming a permanent way of life. Mustering the courage to take on, if not the world, then certainly myself, seemed a stretch too far for me.

That is when I read the story about an ordinary little rabbit called Hazel. He took on the world. And in doing so he allowed me, an ordinary little man, to do the same.

The book is *Watership Down*, by Richard Adams. It changed my life.

I say he was a little rabbit, actually when placed under pressure and when all else seemed lost, he proved to be a massively inspirational, hugely courageous rabbit. He was the Braveheart of the rabbit kingdom.

As I write this I am aware that my statement might sound a little melodramatic – *I read a book about rabbits and I was saved!* But actually, it did change me. I was saved. I was not instantly cleared of shadow – the internal distillation of trapped emotions can take a lifetime – but it did prove to be a turning point in my life.

Let me tell you why the book moved me, and why even today, twenty years further on, just the thought of it still moves me.

Not unusually, the story of *Watership Down* is an allegory; the rabbits represent (to me) mankind and the warren is the world. And Hazel (the story's protagonist), probably the smallest, most insignificant rabbit in the warren, represented me, how I felt about myself at that time and how I felt about my life. In the story Hazel has a psychic brother, Fiver, who foresees the imminent destruction of the Berkshire warren they live in. Trusting Fiver's vision (he is never wrong), Hazel is left with the impossible job of convincing the other rabbits in the warren that they must leave and search for a new, safer home. Hazel is a lower echelon rabbit in the warren hierarchy so, of course, his warning is largely ignored or ridiculed by those above. Only a few of the rabbits heed his warning and leave the warren with him. Most of the rabbits – too arrogant, too scared, too set in their ways – decide to stay exactly where they are and take their chances.

As Fiver had predicted, the warren is destroyed by men with very large tractors (land developers). Hazel and his small band of followers leave just in time. And thus begins their adventure.

And thus began my own adventure; I felt an internal shift when I read of their courage, a pilot light of excitement reignited, a light that had been doused by my fear, and the fear of my family and friends and workmates who had taught me to renounce the adventure of the unknown, and court the comfort of the accepted. I had been weaned in safe warrens; the family, the factory, the same-old, same-old of everyday existence. And that, I believe, is why I was always getting depressed. An intuitive part of me knew that there was a journey to take and that I was the traveller, and that trying to stay safe was actually more dangerous than venturing into the unknown.

Hazel's decision to leave the warren was courageous, not just because he was leaving everything he knew, and not simply because he was trusting in something he could not see (Fiver's premonition), but because in leaving the warren he went against the tide of accepted opinion. This made him an individual, and that takes more courage than that of 1,000 men.

Most people are not even brave enough to have an opinion, let alone act upon a seemingly outrageous vision or take the less-travelled path.

Of course, on their journey there are many opportunities for the rabbits to learn, to grow and to develop their courage (and they are not going to do that from the comfort of their warren); when Hazel takes on a cat in a farmyard face-off I was Hazel. When the terrifying and charismatic General Woundwort (the story's antagonist) takes on a dog in the field ('What's the matter with you? It's just a dog!') I thought, 'I want to be that brave.' And when Bigwig, one of Hazel's converts, takes on General Woundwort in a tunnel fight that was as inspirational as it was epic, my hair stood on end.

The subsequent challenges that are thrust upon our buccaneering rabbits happen (seemingly) every other page before they find their nirvana, Watership Down.

This book single-handedly poked a hole through the darkness of my depression and allowed light to rush into it. I found it so inspirational that I actually wanted to be a rabbit.

Of course, that is not possible (not in this incarnation) so I went for second best. I became a writer.

When I read this book I was a young man that desperately wanted to become a writer. I was in a safe warren (my marriage, my job, my life) but I knew innately that if I didn't vacate, disaster was coming. Looking back, this book inspired my first step away from the known and the ordinary and the safe. And one step led to two steps and two to three, and before I knew it I was running, and searching and (yes) buccaneering.

Many of my old (rabbit) friends did not take the journey with me, and that made the move all the scarier; however, I figure that *scary* is where the adventure is to be had, and if you follow the adventure you are bound to find your own Watership Down. I did.

Chapter 24

The Left-hand Path

When I was younger I used to look at my martial arts heroes and think, 'Why are they so good at what they do? How did they get that good?'

It was only several decades later when I had reached the same heady platform that I understood: these were not players trying to squeeze professional results out of recreational hours. These were men and women who had chosen (yes, chosen) to make martial arts an employ. It was their job.

When they ran five miles early in the morning, it was part of their job.

When they worked the punch bag for an hour a day, it was their work.

When they pushed weights, when they taught classes and when they scrimmaged on the judo mat it was their nine to five.

At some point during their life they took the decision to give up conventional work in order to perfect their martial art.

That is how they got so good.

If you imagine taking the eight hours (or ten or more) that you normally apportion to work, and placing that juicy chunk of time into playing guitar, or writing or sculpting or perfecting a martial art, how could you not get good? How could you not become great? And if you add to the equation *ascending instruction* how could you not, on forty hours a week invested into your passion, become world-class?

When I tell people this, when I inform them that I gave up my job to train full-time in the martial arts, that I later gave up martial arts to write books full-time, and that later still I sidelined book writing to develop myself as a full-time screen writer, they look at me as though I have just pissed on their boots, as though the very concept of eschewing conventional employment to follow a passion is unrealistic. But how can it be unrealistic? It is being done. I am not saying, 'I'm thinking of doing it.' I did it, I am doing it still, I will continue to do it in the future.

This is a matter of record. It is a historical fact.

But I have responsibilities they say, *I have children.*

I had responsibilities. I had four children. All of them at school.

But I have a wife!

Really? What a coincidence, me too (or should I say me two).

What about my mortgage?

What about mine?

Look, I'm not saying that it is easy to be a full-time passion chaser, and I am certainly not saying *do it now! This very minute, in one brave and fell swoop.* I am not saying that. Not at all. That can work, and the in-at-the-deep-end approach suits some, even if it does not suit all. Most make the transition from paid employment to their passion-project gradually, increasing their commitment to the passion as they decrease their hours at work. I was thirty years old before I gave up (what is known in mythology as) *the right-hand path* of convention for the *left-hand path* of danger and excitement. And I didn't do it in one go. It took me three attempts before I could finally let go of a regular wage and earn my living teaching martial arts. It was scary (exciting). I nearly filled my nappy on more than one occasion when I thought I might not make the mortgage. But, man, I have to tell you when I finally did make the transition proper and made my passion my employ it was amazing. I was running down the road at six in the morning thinking, 'This is my job!' I was sparring with my mates thinking, 'This is my work!' I was pushing weights, and training folk, and studying world martial arts from books, tapes and magazines thinking, 'This is what I do for my living.' And I also have to tell you (simply have to) that when I started training full-time, eating, drinking and sleeping the stuff my standard went up faster than a rocket. And this was no lottery, this was no stroke of luck, this was a choice – my choice. I made a decision, I took action and I initiated a life change that still thrills me to this day. I have not worked a conventional job for over fifteen years. It was (still is) like being set free from a long prison term. And all the time I just kept thinking, 'Why isn't everyone doing this?'

Of course you have to make sure that your passion really is your passion. It needs to be strong; don't forget you will likely be doing it (at least) eight hours a day, five days a week. You have to want it like a drowning man wants air; you have to be positively ravenous for it. And thinking that you are ravenous (watching from the sidelines) is not the same as actually being ravenous.

If you are not sure then I'd say don't give up the day job just yet. And if you think you are sure why not be really brave and give it a try?

You will never know until you do.

Chapter 25

Small Profundities

I sat with Sharon over a cup of tea in an early morning cafe where cooked breakfasts sizzled on a hot grill and the elderly queued for a discount meal. At the time I was halfway through writing a film and was trying to impress upon my girl how important it was that I got the screenplay into production so that I could serve people on a global scale. She leaned across the table with some urgency, firmly gripped my hands with hers as though to anchor her words and said, 'Geoff, when you spend half an hour on the phone talking a stranger through his depression, *that* is global.'

How wonderful. How profound. And how very true!

Sometimes we are so busy trying to save the world that we fail to see opportunities to save souls 9 inches in front of us. We are so intent on trying to save a small village in India that we fail to answer the letters sat in our in-tray from people actually asking to be saved. Sometimes we are so busy being public (and large) with our concern for humankind that we ignore, we neglect and we overlook human beings. Sometimes the best way to think (and effect) global is to act local.

Chapter 26

Looking for the Ampersand

I'd spent the best part of a year working on a new book, from conception right through to a bound copy in a display window at Waterstone's, Oxford Street, London. I was proud of my creation. Proud of the tenacity demanded to convert ephemeral thought into a lasting manifest; sitting down for countless hours, pressing the wine of new words from the grape of sun-ripened ideas, forming the visible from the purely metaphysical. I'd spent thousands of hours developing the ideas, hundreds more writing them into an order that pleased the senses, and dozens on top of that re-writing, having taken notes from editors. After no little industry the book found form and went out into the world and... I got a letter (or letters) from a reader(s) informing me (in a vexed undertone) that

136

on page nine, paragraph four, line three, I missed a vital ampersand! The correspondence verily continued with a list of other typos and small (almost wafer thin) grammatical errors and the suggestion (patronising/angry) that *you really ought to get a good editor before going to print*. The presumption being, of course, that I don't use an editor (or if I do, not a good one), and that I lack that professional edge.

Anyway, it happens. Not just on the one book, it happens on a lot of them. Articles too. And films! Well meaning (read *angry*) people are positively insulted by the fact that half a dozen words out of the 70,000 that I penned were (are) spelt incorrectly, used incorrectly or completely unnecessary in the context that I employed them.

Everyone (it would seem) is a critic. Or everyone is a budding part-time (aspiring) editor (or perhaps closet writer?).

I don't mind (honestly!). I have produced and published 40 books. They have left my nest and they have gone on to fly solo in the world.

In the early days I did find it a little semantic, a tad tedious, a small part of me wanted to scream (via letter; I am English, let's keep this respectable) *it's an ampersand for fuck's sake! What about the life changing, bleeding edge words that I have cut a vein for?!*

Of course, I didn't. You don't, do you? It would not be civilised. So I stood back from my angry

(Freudian/defensive) *riposte* and thought *hold on, I could learn something here. Something vital.* And it is not the importance of the ampersand on page nine, line three or the misspelling on page twenty-three, line ten. That's the semantics of the situation, and if I can, if you are not offended, I will leave the semantics to the pedantic. No my friends, my comrades, *mes amis*, what my erstwhile, eagle-eyed editors taught me more than that, much more, was the beautiful art of *finding without looking*.

Let me elaborate.

Always, between my first draft and the final print-ready copy, my book will be read, self-edited, re-read, edited and then re-written literally dozens of times. Its pages will fall open before the eyes of, probably, three highly capable, completely credible professional editors who will spend eight hours a day scanning the manuscript at all its various stages for errors and amendments. Once the book is finally completed the sacred *locked text* will come back to me and the chief editor for one last look before going to print. Even at the print stage I will get sent proofs of the book to check and double check before signing off for the print proper. All of us, everyone, diligently checks for errors. But here lies the gist of my story; we look so hard that we often don't see. Because the moment the book comes out I can guarantee the mail and *errors found* messages that will land on my doorstep.

And this is the exciting bit.

The people that spot the errors that we have so patently missed only spot them because they are not looking. They're just reading the book for enjoyment, not for homework, and yet the errors stand proud from the page as though they are written in large type and underscored in bold. What I love about this is the fact that it draws startling similarities to life, to business and to success. All of my great ideas always come when I am not deliberately looking for them. All my sparks of inspiration occur when I take my mind away from the search.

In Taoism this would be called *the art of searching without searching* (or wu-wei – *doing without doing*). Often we search so hard for the wood of a great idea that we fail to see the trees (and trees and trees) of amazing innovations right in front of our face.

Since this discovery I have stopped looking so hard for inspiration and genius in order to allow inspiration and genius to present themselves to me when they are red and ripe and ready to fall off the tree.

So thank you all you goggle-eyes with your penchant for minutiae – you have taught me nothing about grammar and spelling and the correct placement of the ampersand, but you have taught me much about worthier endeavours that are awaiting my attention (or my non-attention as it were!).

Chapter 27

Writer

When other kids at school were writing three lines in their English books I was filling fifteen pages with my pre-teen thoughts. I was a face full of smiles.

At twelve years it was my stories that got read out in the classroom, and the teacher doffed his cap in my direction.

By sixteen – still at school – I had written and performed in my first short film. It played in front of the whole school and people laughed in all the right places.

In my early twenties I had a poem published and it felt like the cork-popping start to a literary supernova.

Then nothing.

Only despondence, a young marriage and a factory job for life.

My pen was full, my ambition overflowing, but my ideas were missing, presumed dead. My page lay as empty as a politician's smile.

I was a writer with nothing to write about.

By my late twenties the weighty ambition I nurtured clashed with my working-class lot that I carried and I was levelled by the subsequent root-bound implosion.

Six months later, depression still pea-soup, as grey as a tax-inspector, I faced a decision: sink in the quicksand of self-pity or go out and find myself a better story.

I became a bouncer. I fought a pitched battle with the forces of depression and class and low self-esteem, and I won some savage stories which I wrote down on reporter's pads. Man, those stories were stacking up – they came quicker than a Tyson right. They formed the bones and sinew of my first book.

I showed it to a friend. Sharon.

I liked her a lot. I trusted her. Some, closer than her in kin, had already double-stamped on my self-esteem, leaving it cowering like a beaten dog. So I was nervous; more heavy critique (especially the unkind stuff) from someone you care for can be crippling, even fatal.

I said, 'Sharon, I want to be a writer.'

She read my heart on paper and said, 'Geoff, you already *are* a writer.'

I have loved Sharon ever since.

Further Reading

Adams, Richard *Watership Down* (1976, Avon)

Alighieri, Dante *The Divine Comedy: Inferno; Purgatorio; Paradiso* (1995, Everyman's Library)

Anonymous *The Bhagavad-gita* (2004, Longman)

Boethius, Ancius *The Consolation of Philosophy* (2003, Penguin Classics)

Chesterton, G. K. *St. Francis of Assisi* (1987, Bantam Doubleday Dell)

Frankl, Victor, E. *Man's Search For Meaning* (1997, Simon & Schuster)

Gurdjieff, G. *Beelzebub's Tales to His Grandson: AND All and Everything* (2000, Penguin)

Hermann, Hesse *Siddhartha* (1981, Bantam Classics)

Hill, Napoleon *Think & Grow Rich* (1987, Ballantine Books)

Maltz, Maxwell *Psycho-Cybernetics, A New Way to Get More Living Out of Life* (1989, Pocket)

Milton, John *Paradise Lost* (2004, OUP Oxford)

Mitchell, Stephen *Tao Te Ching* (1992, Harper Perennial)

Thompson, Geoff *Watch My Back* (2001, Summersdale Publishers)

Yogananda, Paramahansa *Autobiography of a Yogi* (1946, Self-Realization Fellowship)

Have you enjoyed this book? If so, why not write a review on your favourite website?

Thanks very much for buying this Summersdale book.

www.summersdale.com

www.geoffthompson.com